WITHDRAWN

&

AN UNCENSORED INTRODUCTION

by Nikol Hasler

with illustrations by Michael Capozzola

ZEST BOOKS
San Francisco

AUTHOR ACKNOWLEDGMENTS

I would never have been able to compile the accurate and useful information found in this book without the support of Cory Silverberg, Heather Corrina, Judith Steinhart, Dr. Jeffrey Klausner, Morty Diamond, Tristan Toramino, and Miriam Kaufman. These people took time out of their busy sexual education lives to answer every question I had and are pioneers in the world of sexual information. Through the process they made sure my email inbox stayed interesting with subject lines like "penis queries" and "condoms in butts."

I also want to thank Zest Books publisher Hallie Warshaw for deciding that it was important to write a book like this one and editorial director Karen Macklin for being patient with me during every step of the process. Also thanks to Zest's research editor Nikki Roddy, who spent an awful lot of time looking at lengthy documents and pie charts on everything from bodily fluids to penis sizes.

Most important, I want to thank my sons for interrupting me every now and then to show me that a good hour of silly dancing in the kitchen can be an excellent cure for just about anything. —NIKOL HASLER

This is a revised and expanded edition of *Sex: A Book for Teens* (Zest Books, 2010). This new edition includes an additional chapter on the topic of online sex and safety, along with updated information about new legislation, medical discoveries, and cultural shifts — especially on the topic of transgender issues. It also includes a fully updated resources section.

Connect with Zest!

- zestbooks.net/blog   - twitter.com/zestbooks
- zestbooks.net/contests - facebook.com/BooksWithATwist

35 Stillman Street, Suite 121, San Francisco, CA 94107 / www.zestbooks.net

Manufactured in the U.S.A.
DOC 10 9 8 7 6 5 4 3 2 1
4500514214

CONTENTS

INTROD

You've probably already figured this out from the title, but the book you are holding in your hands right now is about sex. That's right. It takes the two most exciting things in the world — sex and books — and combines them into this one magnificent object. Yep, every word, sentence, and illustration in this book is about that three-letter word that everyone is thinking about on some level or another — even if they don't want to admit it. So, why a book about sex? And, more important, why *this* book about sex?

From a very early age I received a lot of mixed-up information about sex. Family members, friends, teachers, the media — everyone had opinions about what was okay and normal, bad and strange. As a kid, you rely on other people to help you make sense of things, and when everyone seems to be at odds with one topic, it can make that topic difficult to talk about. Like everything in my life that ever confused me, I dealt with sex by cracking a lot of jokes about it.

Still, by the age of 18, I was pregnant and homeless and still absolutely confused about sex. Was I a bad person for wanting it? Was I a bad girlfriend if I didn't? What was the point of safe sex, really? How could I tell someone that I wasn't interested in having sex? Was I gay? Was I normal? Would I ever be?

In 2007, I began making a web series with my friends, and it was through that series that I was finally able to talk to that teenage version of myself and say things that would have made a difference to hear. We insisted on keeping it funny and ridiculous because life is funny and

UCTION

ridiculous. Now the mother of teens, I talk to them about everything the same way I talk to all of you in this book. This is my conversation with you, only you don't get to say anything back to me. Sorry. (Also, if we were talking face to face we probably wouldn't spend the whole time talking about sex. Only about 80 percent...)

But there's only so much we can say in three-minute-long webisodes, which is why I wanted to write this book.

There is an awful lot of information out there about sex, and it is pretty easy to access. And yet teens are still getting pregnant, picking up sexually transmitted infections, and learning about sex through information that is incorrect, condescending, or just plain boring. There's nothing boring about sex, so why should you feel bored while learning about it?

This book is about everything that has to do with sex: bodies, birth control, virginity, sexual orientation, masturbation, dating, sexually transmitted infections, performance, orgasms, what to do if you're in love with a werewolf and your friends don't approve... This book is not here to tell you to have or not to have sex — it's to tell you what you need to know if you are having sex, or ever will. Everyone has questions about sex, even those who aren't "doing it" yet. Even people who have been doing it for a bajillion years still have questions (like, why am I still alive and having sex as a bajillion-year old?).

I love humor. But I also believe in supremely factual and up-to-date info, so I consulted many doctors and sex experts to write this book. I have also included a great list of teen resources at the end, so you can find answers to anything this book doesn't cover and get new information when it comes out.

Any book about sex is going to need to be updated from time to time. Updated information comes to light, new technologies are introduced, and the medical field fixes things that once held us back. This book was initially written as a result of that web series I hosted in 2007. At the time, there was nothing else like it. Shortly after that, web videos started to boom, and now the amount of people out there talking openly about sex is immeasurable. In this updated version, we introduce a whole new chapter focusing on that technology and added some great bits of new information about a few things that have changed. (You could make it a game. Read the old one and then find the changes. I didn't say it was a fun game. But maybe you live someplace really boring and you're too old to play Mouse Trap.)

Now, on to the book! Read it. Get your friends to read it. Talk about it. Put the words into song. Buy two copies and compare them to see if there are any differences. Wildly wave your copy in the air and quote parts of it in the hallways. Or... just read it. But then take the information you've gleaned and do something useful with it, like understand your body more and figure out how to talk about sex. And remember that it is OK to laugh. After all, sex is a serious topic, but it's also pretty funny.

— Nikol Hasler, writer and host
of the *Midwest Teen Sex Show*

CHAPTER 1

YOUR BODY

How It Works and How to Treat It

When talking about sex, the best place to begin is by taking a close look at your body. That may sound like a given, but lots of people ignore their bodies — or have no idea what the different parts do — and then they get freaked out when seemingly weird (but really perfectly normal) things happen.

This chapter is not about how your heart and lungs work because that would be boring (and no book about sex should start out boring!). But here is a good rundown of the sexual body parts, how they function, and how to keep them in good working order. And remember: It's also important to learn about other people's bodies. Even if you don't have a penis or a vagina, you should still become familiar with how one works — especially if you plan on getting intimate with one at some point.

YOUR REPRODUCTIVE ORGANS

These body parts are some of the most interesting ones you have (despite their odd, medical-sounding names). Even if you think you know the 411 on what they all do, here's a quick review.

FEMALE REPRODUCTIVE PARTS

Girls have a lot of small parts, each of which serves a different purpose. People often just call the whole area the vagina, but most of it is technically called the vulva (see below). The mons pubis is the mound of fatty tissue, skin, and pubic hair that sits over the pubic bone. The vulva is the area that contains all of the external female genitalia, including the labia majora, labia minora, clitoris, clitoral hood, urethral opening, and the vaginal opening. The labia majora (or outside lips) and the labia minora (inside lips) are the two pairs of skin folds and help protect what's inside. The clitoris is a knob-like bundle of nerves. Stimulation of the clitoris during sexual activity causes girls to be sexually excited and to have orgasms. The little flap on top of it is the clitoral hood.

Below the clitoris is the urethral opening, where urine comes out. It is the place where the urethra begins. The urethra is the tube that leads to your bladder, which sits right below the ovaries and against the cervix.

Below the urethral opening is the introitus, or vaginal opening, which leads to the muscular canal known as the vagina. This is the birth canal.

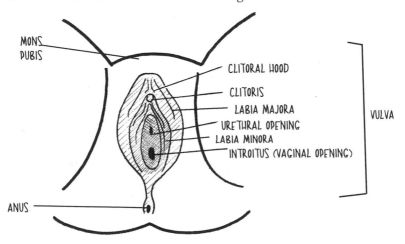

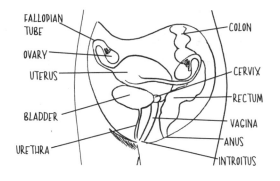

FALLOPIAN TUBE
OVARY
UTERUS
BLADDER
URETHRA
COLON
CERVIX
RECTUM
VAGINA
ANUS
INTROITUS

It is also where period blood comes out, and where tampons and certain forms of birth control go in. During sex, it is where the penis (or fingers) are inserted.

Beyond the vagina is the cervix. The cervix is located at the lower, narrow portion of the uterus, where the uterus joins with the top end of the vagina. The uterus is where a baby will grow during a normal pregnancy. The fallopian tubes link the uterus to the ovaries, which house all of the eggs — the little seeds for babies. (All girls are born with all of the eggs they'll ever have.) To understand how all of this functions in the baby-making process, go to page 13.

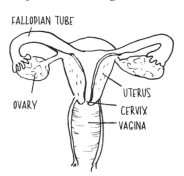

FALLOPIAN TUBE
OVARY
UTERUS
CERVIX
VAGINA

WHAT'S THAT WHITE STUFF?

You may have noticed that the vagina produces a discharge. It's usually normal and helps keep the vagina clean and moist, as well as prevent and fight off infections. It's normal for the color, texture, and amount of your vaginal discharge to change throughout the month. It can be thin and sticky, or thick and gooey, and the normal colors are clear, white, or slightly off-white. However, if you ever experience a change in odor (like a strong, fishy odor), change in color (greenish or grayish), vaginal itching, burning, or swelling, or bleeding when not on your period, contact your doctor or a clinic immediately. It may be an indicator of something funky going on with your vaginal health, like bacterial or fungal problems, or sexually transmitted infections (which you can read more about in Chapter 7).

MALE REPRODUCTIVE PARTS

Unlike a girl's reproductive parts, which are tucked inside the body, a guy's sex organs are both inside and outside. The parts on the outside are the penis and the scrotum. The penis is made up of the shaft and the glans (aka the head). Inside the penis is a tube called the urethra; it is through this tube that both semen and urine travel and then exit through a small opening at the tip of the glans, called the urethral opening. The scrotum is a handy little sac that hangs below the penis and contains the testicles, which are two oval-shaped glands that produce sperm cells (male sex cells that look kind of like tadpoles.

After the sperm is created in the testicles, it moves through a set of coiled tubes called the epididymis, and then up through a long tube called the vas deferens to the seminal vesicles, which are glands behind the bladder. Here, the sperm mixes with fluid that is produced by the seminal vesicles. Then this mixture goes to the prostate (a little gland that sits below the bladder), where it mixes again with more fluid and, when a guy ejaculates, is eventually propelled out of the urethral opening in that

THE BIOLOGY OF BONERS

A boner, erection, hard on, or stiffy usually starts with the brain. You either see, think about, or feel something that gets you sexually aroused and your brain sends an "Oh, yeah!" message to your penis, telling the blood vessels to open up. Blood rushes in at a faster rate that it can flow out, trapping the blood in the penis and causing it to get longer and harder, creating a boner. But note: Even though people call it a boner, there aren't any actual bones in a penis.

Of course, there are those not-so-cool spontaneous erections you occasionally get without thinking about anything sexual at all, like during math class. These can be embarrassing but are par for the course when it comes to raging teenage hormones. Guys also sometimes wake up with erections (aka morning wood) or have boners and ejaculate while sleeping (read more about this on page 47), both of which are also totally normal.

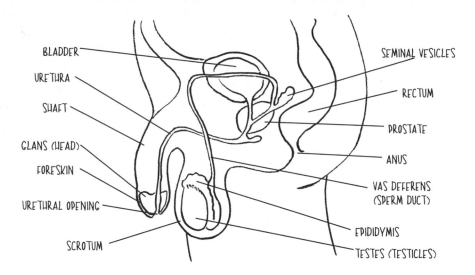

BLADDER

URETHRA

SHAFT

GLANS (HEAD)

FORESKIN

URETHRAL OPENING

SCROTUM

SEMINAL VESICLES

RECTUM

PROSTATE

ANUS

VAS DEFERENS (SPERM DUCT)

EPIDIDYMIS

TESTES (TESTICLES)

white sticky stuff called semen. Because the penis and the scrotum live outside the body, they are sensitive to temperature changes. They both tend to get smaller when it is cold outside — this is to regulate the temperature of the testicles and protect the sperm inside.

WHEN SPERM MEETS EGG

Most of you probably know by now how babies are made, but just in case you've been getting your sex education from the writing on the bathroom wall — or from that cousin who knows nothing about everything — here's a quick lesson.

Every month an egg (or two) makes its way into one of the fallopian tubes where it waits for a few days for a handsome sperm to arrive and try to get inside. Many sperm are competing for this egg, and the strongest, fastest swimmer will win. (The sperm are inside the ejaculation of the guy with whom the girl is having sex.) If a sperm makes it to the egg, it will try to fertilize it, and if it does, that egg will then move to the girl's uterus, where it will find a spot to attach itself, and a baby will start to grow. If the egg does not get fertilized, it gets reabsorbed by the body and the now-unneeded blood and tissue — which made up the lining of the uterus to nourish the baby and provide a nice, cushy place for it to grow — will now leave the body. The blood that comes out is a girl's period (more about this on pages 18-19).

CIRCUMCISED OR NOT?

When boys are born, their parents may choose to have them circumcised. This involves removing the foreskin, which is a retractable layer of skin that covers the urethra when a boy doesn't have a boner. The decision to be circumcised can be made later in life, as well. Some reasons that people choose circumcision are religious, health, or wanting the child's penis to look like his father's. Some men decide to have their foreskin removed because they don't like the way it looks. And, in some rare cases, circumcised men will try to have their foreskin restored later on in life, though that type of surgery is not yet very effective.

CIRCUMCISED PENIS

UNCIRCUMCISED PENIS

One way or the other, a penis is still a penis and it works just the same. If you do have a foreskin, you need to be sure to pull the skin back and clean the skin underneath on a regular basis. But anyone with any sort of penis should be cleaning it anyway.

YOUR NEW BODY

Puberty. You are probably in some stage of it right now and know that it's a time when your body is going through all sorts of changes — some of which are cool and some of which are, well, kind of strange.

For guys, the big changes are that their testicles and scrotums grow larger, their penises grows longer, and their voices deepen. Meanwhile, girls' breasts take shape, their nipples change color and size, their vaginas take on new shapes, coloration, and smells, and they get their periods. And both guys and girls get new body hair — and pimples.

The thing is that people don't really want to talk about puberty. Guys don't have group meetings at cafés to discuss the arrival of pubic hair, and a lot of girls are still embarrassed about their periods, as if carrying a tampon is akin to smuggling illegal drugs. But even if you're not talking about it, you know that it's going on.

WHAT'S NORMAL?

While some people's bodies develop before they are even teens, others may not finish developing until after high school. And for some people, the changes to their bodies seem to happen in just a year; others experience the changes more slowly and gradually. This inconsistency in development freaks out some people. Boys may wonder if their penises are too small (unlikely), too big (really unlikely), or just curved weird, while girls start sweating the size of their boobs, which can range from two little bumps to cleavage factories. It's hard, but try not to get too caught up comparing what your body is doing as opposed to everyone else's.

If you are worrying about whether the sizes and appearances of your newly developed parts are normal, rest assured that almost all are. Here are some stats to make you feel better.

WHAT'S IN A NAME?

Although we've mostly been keeping to the basics, there are lots of great (and not so great) names for your body parts! Here are some of our faves.

- **Breasts:** airbags, tits, bee bites, balcony, charleys, boo-boos, tittybojangles, tracks of land, chesticles, headlights, knockers, boobies, fun bags, dairy pillows

- **Penis:** one-eyed trouser snake, schlong, purple-headed yogurt slinger, dong, wang, wienie, baby arm, dome piece, jimber, Mr. Happy, plonker, tallywacker, manhandle, tubesteak, dick, throbber, knob, tool, donger, putz, winkle, pork sword
- **Scrotum:** bagpipes, crip, fruitbowl, hangy-down bits, lamel, soapbox, webbos, nads, nuts, the boys, balls, plums, eggs, man berries, lads in the bag, the twins

- **Vagina:** kitty, coochie, honey pot, cha cha, flange, poon, lala, lady garden, minge, quim, tunnel of love, vertical smile, vagoo, beaver, box, bald man in a boat, pink taco, va-jay-jay

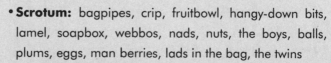

- **Penises.** These come in all different sizes, with the average male penis being 5 – 6.5 inches when hard. The size it is while flaccid (meaning soft) varies a lot and actually has nothing to do with what size it grows to when it's excited. Some guys like to think of penises in terms of "growers" or "showers" (the first type is small when flaccid, but gets much bigger when hard; the second type is big when flaccid and grows comparitively less when hard).

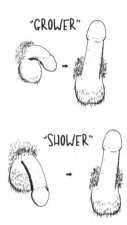

- **Breasts.** These range from size AAs to L (that's six sizes larger than triple Ds). Size is determined by all different kinds of factors, including genetics, weight, body size, and personal hormones. Breasts have typically finished growing when girls are about 17, but some girls report really "popping out" as late as college.
- **Nipples.** These can be anywhere from pink to brown, bumpy to smooth, and small to (in some cases) almost the same size as the entire breast. They can even be inverted, which is when nipples go inward like an innie belly button. Some girls may also notice bumps on their nipples — don't get squeezy with them. They aren't pimples, just naturally occurring bumps that help keep nips moisturized — everyone needs a good moisturizer.
- **Vulvas.** These vary in color and size, with the labia minora (the inside "lips" — see illustration on page 10) ranging in color from pink to red to brown, purple, or even gray. Sometimes the lips are small, and sometimes they seem to hang down pretty low. Vulvas are like snowflakes — no two look the same.

WHAT'S THAT SMELL?

So, as you've probably noticed, one thing that happens as your body matures is that it takes on all sorts of new and interesting smells. And you've probably noticed that your body isn't the only one. Hormones are at work, and it's totally normal. Here's a list of body parts that could potentially get stinky, and some ways to deal.

- **Underarms.** Deodorant is a fabulous idea because it gets rid of the odor of sweat by covering it up. Sometimes it comes with antiperspirant, which actually stops sweat from coming out. (Some people don't like to use antiperspirant because they'd rather allow their bodies to get that sweat out in order to remove toxins from the system.) Both deodorant-only products and those with antiperspirants can be found at the drugstore.
- **Penises and scrotums.** If you don't like the way things smell down there, staying clean is the best antidote. Wash your penis with a mild soap, being careful not to get any soap inside your pee hole. You can also use an unscented powder to keep the sweat from creating a stench.
- **Vaginas.** If you are the proud owner of a vagina, you should know that mature vaginas naturally have a strong smell. Not a bad smell, but a very distinctive smell, which is part of what makes it a vagina. Embrace it! The best way to keep it smelling nice is to simply stay clean. You don't need anything special — simply water or a very mild soap. Don't make the mistake of using scented and strong soaps to clean your dainty parts because these can irritate you. Also, never use douches. Douching (the name comes from the French word for "wash") refers to washing out the vagina, usually with a prepackaged mix of fluids. Douching, along with using feminine sprays and vaginal deodorants, is a bad idea. These things can lead to allergic reactions, irritations, and infections that can throw off the balance of your vag, which will retaliate by smelling bad instead of just smelling normal.

GIMME HAIR

Now that you're a teenager, you've got new hair to deal with in all sorts of places — and some of it you may not want seen by the general public.

Girls often remove hair from multiple areas, like their underarms, legs, and pubic areas. Guys often remove hair from their faces, and it is

WHY IS IT SO DARK?

The hair you grow on your body is not the same as the hair on your head. And thank goodness. Can you imagine how much of a hassle it would be to keep up with that much hair in your crotch? While some people have light-colored pubic hair, most have dark-brown to black pubes that are coarse and curly, and a lot darker than the hair on the top of their head. This comes as a shock to anyone expecting the "drapes to match the carpet."

becoming more common for them to also shave other parts of their bodies, such as their chests, backs, and even scrotums.

Depending on where you want to get rid of hair and how much there is to get rid of, there are many hair-removal options: waxing, shaving, depilatories, plucking, and a laser.

If you choose to remove hair, make sure you are doing it based on your own desires and not because someone else is telling you what your body is supposed to look like.

PERIODS

It's inevitable. If you are a girl, you are going to have a period. And if you are reading this book, there is a very good chance that you already do. But do you know exactly what it is? As mentioned on page 13, a period (or menstruation) happens when the lining inside a girl's uterus is shed. The lining builds up each month to be a cushion for a baby, and if there is no baby (the egg doesn't get fertilized), the lining comes out. This lining consists of blood, tissue, and mucus, but it basically looks like blood. It can be bright red, dark red, or even brown, and it sometimes has clots in it. This shedding usually happens over the course of three to six days, and though it's a pretty fascinating thing that your body does, it can also suck. That's because it often comes with things like cramping in your lower belly, lower back pain, tenderness and puffiness in your boobs, bloating, crankiness, and acne flare-ups.

This stuff can be helped out by a little ibuprofen, light exercise, healthy eating, lower back rubs, warm baths, rest, and patience. If you find yourself craving foods that are greasy or fatty, it is OK to indulge a little bit. Just don't overdo it.

It's normal to be abit on the emotional side, as well. If you tend to get sad or angry before or during your period, try to stay away from people or activities that stress you out. Also, even though you can do everything you normally would, it's also good to cut yourself some slack on the first couple of days and take it easy — especially if you are bleeding heavily or experiencing a lot of cramps.

For the first few years that you have your period it may not be regular, meaning that its arrival is unpredictable. There you are, minding your own business in history class and all of a sudden you have your own battle

PADS OR TAMPONS?

Pads and tampons are the favored ways to deal with all that monthly blood-letting. It's best to try out both and see which works best for you. As you probably already know, pads (aka sanitary napkins) stick to your underwear and absorb the blood as it comes out. Tampons are typically tightly packed cylinders of cotton (or other fibers) that go inside of your vagina. Read the instructions on the tampon box to learn how to put one in (or ask your mom or a friend for tips). They come in a variety of sizes based on the heaviness of your flow (use the smallest one you need), and they either have applicators or can be inserted with your finger.

Pads are great for girls who don't want to stick anything in there quite yet, but tampons are a period victory because they make it easier to play sports, swim, and dance around to your favorite song without worrying about your pad landing on the floor. Pads should be changed at least every three to four hours or when they are full of blood. Tampons should be changed every four to eight hours depending on your flow. It is really important to stick to this schedule for both health and sanitary reasons. When you do change your tampon or pad, don't flush it down the toilet. Wrap it in toilet paper and put it in the garbage can. Most septic systems cannot handle sanitary products, and the last thing you want to have to deal with is flooding the school or a restaurant with your maxi pad.

wound. Don't let this make you forever associate the Gettysburg Address with an annoying situation. Lincoln may not have cured PMS, but he did some pretty great things. Your body usually gets adjusted to a schedule after a while, but some girls never have regular periods because of things ranging from nutrition to exercise to wacky hormones. Your period may also be three days long one month and eight days long the next. If you are concerned about irregular periods, ask your doc what she thinks. She might put you on a birth control pill, which will regulate your periods, or she might just tell you not to worry about it.

Sometimes you might bleed in between your periods. This is called spotting. If this happens to you, unless there's a large amount of blood loss or you're in pain, you don't need to panic and rush to the emergency room. You do need to see your doctor. Again, there may not be anything to worry about, but spotting can be the result of something more serious, so you should rule out anything that might be amiss.

Your period is actually pretty cool. It's a sign that you are healthy, not pregnant, and ready to start a new month. There's no point in being embarrassed about it — it's a normal bodily function. And if you are a boy and you are all sicked out at the thought of periods, try to keep that mentality to yourself. You wouldn't want the girls making jokes about your occasional boners, so let them bleed in peace.

AT THE DOCTOR

Doctors have been examining your body since the day you were born to make sure everything is in working order. As you get older, this routine exam loses its fun factor. (You probably won't even get a lollipop when you're done.) But the health benefits are worth the little bit of awkwardness or discomfort.

LADIES EXAM

If you are a girl, you'll probably start seeing a doctor for your reproductive health some time after you hit puberty, between ages 14 and 17. These visits consist of breast and pelvic exams, as well as consultations about birth control and the prevention of STIs (sexually transmitted infections). Visits are especially important if you are sexually active, want to start taking some sort of birth control, or have any concerns about your periods. These days, a lot of family doctors do these types of checkups, so you could

SPECULUM
(AKA DUCK'S BILL)

potentially just see your regular doctor, or you could go to a gynecologist, which is a doctor specially trained in women's health issues.

After giving you a breast exam to check for any lumps or abnormalities, the doctor will begin the pelvic exam. For this, you will lay on an exam table wearing a hospital gown-type thing, which is not high fashion but sometimes has pretty floral prints. You will put your feet into two metal rests called stirrups. The doctor will start by looking at the folds of your vulva and the openings of your vagina, checking for any signs of cysts, an irregular discharge, warts, or other conditions. The doctor will then insert a speculum into your vagina (a metal thing that looks like a duck's bill) to open it up a teeny bit and get a look inside.

The doc will look at your cervix to make sure there are no abnormalities and use a long, narrow, small spatula and a small brush to take a cell sample, which will usually be put in a vial of fluid to be sent to a lab. This is called a Pap smear, and the purpose of this test is to check for any pre-cancerous cells in the cervix (very unlikely at your age, but better safe than sorry). If you are sexually active, tell the doctor, as he or she may also want to swab for STIs during this part of the exam.

Then the doc will remove the speculum and use his or her fingers to feel inside your vagina and push against your lower belly to feel your ovaries. This is done to make sure that your organs are developing normally. It is rarer, but a doc may also put a finger inside your rectum. This checks to see if there are tumors behind the uterus, on the lower wall of the vagina, or in the rectum. If you are uncomfortable, it is good to let your doctor know. They still need to do the exam, but it can make you feel better to tell them. Also, if they know you are nervous, they can be extra gentle and more comforting.

GENTS EXAM

If you are a guy, it's a much easier situation. Unless there is something strange going on, you won't need to go to a special doctor — just your general one. Along with your routine exam, he or she will feel your testicles and penis to make sure they are developing normally, and to check for anything out of the ordinary, like abnormal cell growth that could mean a cancerous tumor.

If you get sexually excited during the exam, try not to feel too embarrassed. It's natural to get aroused when someone is touching your penis. Of course, if you are sexually active, you must tell your doctor, as she or he may want to do some STI tests. These tests used to mean a not-so-pleasant swab of the urethra for boys, but today it usually just means a blood or urine test. Easy.

LOVE YOUR BODY

So now you know the ins and outs of your reproductive anatomy. But how do you feel about how you actually look? If you're like lots of teens, you're probably not totally satisfied with your body. But that's an attitude that comes from reading all of those "Top Ten Ways to Be Hotter Than Hot" advice columns and "Hottest People of All Time" lists. There is no single definition of good-looking, and you should learn to love your body, because it's awesome and it's the only one you have (unless you have some sort of crazy superpower and can morph into other shapes, which would be cool until someone dragged you off to a scientific testing facility).

If you are doubting whether or not you are good-looking in someone else's eyes, remember that all people are attracted to different things. By

BREAST AUGMENTATION

If you're a girl with big breasts, you might love them — or hate them. Girls with larger breasts sometimes report back pain and discomfort, and, despite what some may think, the extra attention that big boobs command is not always wanted. In these cases, girls sometimes opt for a breast reduction. Breast reductions are generally standard and safe, and large-breasted women often report feeling lighter and freer after downsizing. Other candidates for breast reductions are women with unevenly sized breasts and males who, in rare cases, develop breasts.

If you're a girl with small breasts, you might think that you just don't size up. But do not rush off to get a consult with a plastic surgeon. *Please.* Breast enlargements come with sizable risks and dangers, so it's not a decision to be made lightly. Most teen girls feel somehow dissatisfied with their body parts. But give yourself a few years — you may decide, at 25, that you absolutely love having size As!

Also remember that unless you have a physician (and not just a plastic surgeon) who recommends that you have surgery, you need to wait until your breasts are fully grown before getting any type of breast enlargement.

now, you may even realize this, noticing that you are attracted to girls with glasses and straight hair or to boys with lanky legs or broad shoulders. Even a small thing like the shape of an earlobe can be a point of attraction. So when you think about your own attractiveness to others, remember that there are many things beyond a flat belly or perfect skin that can drive a guy/girl wild.

It is good to be concerned with things like staying healthy and active, but it's pretty useless to obsessively think about the parts of you that you cannot change. Confidence is one of the sexiest traits a person can have. The other is being really good at math.

KEEP A HEALTHY WEIGHT

Staying at a healthy weight is important, but lots of people have poor eating, exercise, and lifestyle habits that leave them at unhealthy weights and in big trouble with their bodies.

DEALING WITH OBESITY

You may have noticed that we have a problem with obesity (being seriously overweight) in modern society. Obesity can cause lots of health issues, including heart problems, type 2 diabetes, and sleep apnea (trouble breathing during sleep). It's come to affect more and more teenagers. Why? Because children in our society are eating more fast food and junk food and becoming less active than ever before, and all of this bad diet and inactivity causes them to become obese. Then, obese children turn into obese teenagers. So, what to do?

If you are overweight and want to get a jump-start on staying in shape, pay attention to eating suggested portion sizes. Read food labels to avoid saturated fats, stay far away from fast food, and fit in some regular exercise. This might mean walking to school instead of getting a ride. It could also mean joining a sports team, or putting in the extra effort that your gym teacher has been asking of you.

DIETING TO DEATH

Many girls (and some guys) take the idea of being slim too far and develop eating disorders. The two most well-known types of eating disorders are anorexia and bulimia. Anorexia is when someone restricts what he or she eats to a point close to starvation. Bulimia is when someone has episodes (often secretive) of excessive eating followed by harmful methods of forcing the food out, including vomiting, taking laxatives, and/or over-exercising. These disorders can be very dangerous, and a person can have one of them or both. They are very common and affect 10 in 100 girls in the US. Both can also be deadly. Starving yourself can lead to all kinds of life-threatening complications, and excessive vomiting can eliminate essential electrolytes from the body, putting a lot of strain on the heart, which can cause heart failure. Overeating is also an eating disorder, but its one that doesn't get talked about as often. It's much easier to see someone who is starving herself and think that she's dealing with a mental illness, but society has told us for a long time that if someone is fat, it's her fault. People who binge eat are often too ashamed of themselves to know that they need help or to reach out to get help, but the physical effects are just as dangerous, and the pain is just as real. The only way someone can move past an eating disorder is through getting help, usually from a therapist or support group.

So how do these disorders come about? It depends. In some cases, people with eating disorders see a distorted image of themselves when they look in the mirror and believe they are bigger than they really are. In other cases, the eating disorder represents a way of maintaining control over something in life. Other things — personality traits, environmental factors, and genetics — may also be causes.

If you think you might have an eating disorder, talk to someone about it as soon as possible. It's not a life sentence, and, with the right help, you will get past it. The best thing you can do for a friend with an eating disorder is to be there for him or her. Let them know directly that they need to take steps to help themselves, and be supportive of the recovery, not the disorder. •

Q & A

Q. My friends are all really focused on dieting right now. I never thought I was fat before, but with all of them talking about what size they wear and pinching each other's extra skin I've started to notice that I am bigger than all of them. I heard that you can take laxatives, and some of the girls are taking diet aids. Which of these are safest for me to take?

A. None of them are safe. Taking laxatives to lose weight is completely unhealthy and can lead to problems with your stomach and bowels. Taking diet pills seems like a quick fix, but people can become dependent on those pills. Crash dieting, where you restrict your eating to lose weight fast, will mess with your metabolism and make you put on more weight once you return to even the healthiest of eating habits.

People get a message early in life that in order to be attractive they need to be Hollywood skinny, but that's not true. Talk to your doctor. If she says you're overweight, ask her for some healthy weight-loss ideas. If she agrees that you are of a healthy weight, keep doing what you normally would and try to educate your muffin top-grabbing buddies.

Q. My penis is kind of small. I haven't had sex yet, but I am worried that girls won't want to have sex with me when they see it. Is it true that girls like guys who have big penises better?

A. Some girls do, just as some guys like girls with bigger breasts. But it is a personal preference. Some girls are not into big penises at all. Just like all penises are different in size, vaginas are different in depth, and large penises don't feel good to all girls. Having a less than ginormous shlong is definitely not a sexual death sentence.

The most important thing is that you feel confident about your body. If you psych yourself out by thinking you are too small, your fears will become a turnoff for both of you. So relax and be comfortable with yourself, and you're sure to find a girl who fits with you perfectly.

Q. Our school locker room is totally open, even the showers. It makes things kind of weird because I'm an openly gay kid, and I am really sensitive to guys thinking I want them. They are all snapping towels and making penis jokes, but if I get in the shower they all give me looks and get out. What is the best way to deal with this?

A. This is hard because you are stuck in an uncomfortable situation that, if you weren't in high school, you wouldn't have to remain in. You could make a big point of telling them you don't want to touch their junk and they should just chill out, but naked teenage boys may not handle that too well. You probably need to just go about doing your thing. You have just as much right and need after a long day of relays to shower off the stench, so stay comfortable with yourself and try to keep in mind that they are wrong and you will smell better than them for the rest of the day. Luckily, in four years, you'll no longer have to deal with them.

Q. I am a girl, and I have recently started getting little black hairs on my nipples. Help! Why is this happening to me and how can I make it stop?

A. *You may not want to hear this, but ... you can't make it stop. That is just the way it is. Your hormones are changing and sometimes that means getting nipple hair. It's way more common than you think. Plucking it can irritate the hair follicles around the nipple, so if it really bothers you, just trim it with scissors or go to a dermatologist who can advise you on other forms of hair removal for that area.*

Q. I am really flat-chested. All of my friends are wearing bras, but I don't really need one. Is it OK to just not wear a bra? Can people tell?

A. *Bras are not necessary for the healthy development of breasts. Bras are cool because they offer support for people who want to keep their breasts close to their bodies; can create different looks with padding and underwires; and prevent your nips from making a scene. But if you don't want to deal with one, don't wear one. If you are worried about people noticing your braless ways, try to wear heavy fabrics, as your nipples are more likely to pop out through thinner ones. And keep a few bras around — or even just fitted tanks — in case you want to wear a thin fabric one day or something with big open sleeves. Sports bras are also great for when you play sports or are physically active.*

Q. I am a little overweight and too embarrassed to let my boyfriend see me naked. He says he doesn't care, but I just don't feel confident enough. He asked for some naked pictures of me that he can look at until I feel ready to get intimate with him. I feel more comfortable with this, since I won't be able to see his disappointment if he doesn't like what he sees. But I don't want to send them through my cell phone or online. Can I get into any trouble if I just print them out for him?

A. Yes. Yes you can. More and more law enforcement agencies are cracking down on child pornography, which they classify as any naked or sexual pictures of a person under the age of 18. (More about this on page 174.) Cell phone, online, print — it's all the same. And not only are the teens who are taking the pictures getting into loads of trouble, but whoever has those pictures can also be charged with possession of child pornography and forever be identified as a sex offender. Also, by giving someone a naked photo of yourself, you are taking a really big risk. You and your boyfriend might not stay together forever, and it is not very wise to hand off a picture that could be used against you later.

But the bigger question here is: Why don't you love your body? You should love it regardless of what your boyfriend thinks.

 THERE ARE NO STUPID QUESTIONS — EXCEPT FOR THIS ONE

Q. As a dude, I love touching boobs, but am always striking out with the ladies. Can I get breast implants?

CHAPTER 2

SEXUAL IDENTIFICATION

Who Are You?

S exuality is not just about getting it on. It's also about understanding your sexual orientation (who you are attracted to) and your gender identity (what gender you identify as). For some people, this is all very clear from an early age. You're a guy and you like girls, and you never even think it might be otherwise. For others, it can feel murky and confusing at first. Maybe you are a girl and you like girls, but you don't know if that's OK. Or maybe you are a guy, but you don't truly feel like a guy, and you're not sure why.

Society is just starting to talk more openly about sexual orientation and gender identity, which is good. This means that people are finally understanding that it's OK to be whoever you are and be attracted to whomever you feel attracted to. It's all part of human nature, and it's all normal and great. The important thing is that you feel comfortable with yourself and are also OK with people who are different from you.

WHAT IS SEXUAL ORIENTATION?

Your sexual orientation, or sexual preference, describes who you are sexually attracted to. It's also about who you get all fuzzy around, who you want to date, who you fall in love with — and even who you want to spend your life with. Most people fit into one of these categories: homosexual (people attracted to those of the same sex, aka gay or lesbian), heterosexual (people attracted to those of the opposite sex, aka straight), or bisexual (people attracted to both sexes, aka bi). People who are lesbian, gay, bi, or transgender often identify themselves as LGBT or queer.

So how is sexual orientation determined? Scientists and researchers are still studying this, but most believe it's at least partially decided while you are inside your mom's belly. This doesn't mean you're born ready to have sex (despite what you may brag to your friends). It just means that your sexual preference is being formulated even before you are born. As you grow up, certain environmental factors may also influence your sexuality, and if you are born with the redundant tendency to be attracted to both genders, as many people are, you may find that your sexuality is fluid — meaning that your preferences will change over the course of your life.

STRAIGHT, GAY, OR LESBIAN?

Some people just know from the get-go that they are straight or gay. For others, it can be more confusing — one minute it's one way and the next minute it's another way. High school isn't necessarily the easiest place to figure out your sexuality because the pressure to be a certain way in order to be accepted is so great. Defining your sexual orientation often gets easier as you get older and you will come to better understand yourself in general.

It's important to remember that sexuality is fluid for some people, and preferences can change. So someone might feel straight up until their twenties and then shift and want to date someone of the same gender.

It could also go the other way. It's perfectly fine for you to switch teams throughout the course of your life.

WHAT IF I LIKE BOTH GENDERS?

Those people attracted to both genders (lucky you!) are often considered bisexual. Bisexuality was all the rage in ancient Greece and is a fairly common occurrence these days. While most of us have a strong preference for one sex or the other, many people admit to having had sexual experiences with both genders.

Like anything, your level of bisexuality may change throughout the course of your life, and there may be periods in which you feel more straight or more gay than bisexual. And you may also be using bisexuality to experiment. Even if you are pretty sure you are gay, you might be curious about what straight sex is like. And it is perfectly natural, even if you consider yourself to be totally straight, to find something attractive about someone of your same gender, even if you never act on it. After all, those people have the same parts you live with every day, and you think you're sexy, right?

WHAT IT MEANS TO BE TRANSGENDER

Another thing that some people grapple with, especially as they hit their teen years, is gender. While most biological boys feel more or less like boys and most biological girls feel more or less like girls (regardless of being gay or straight), some people really feel they do not identify with the gender they are given at birth. Some people also identify with more than one gender or do not identify with any gender at all.

Those who take steps to change what they see on the outside to match up with how they feel on the inside generally identify themselves as transgender, which is what the T stands for in LGBT. The word *transgender* (sometimes shortened to trans) is an umbrella term, and some people might use a more specific term to describe themselves like *transman, transwoman,* or *genderqueer.* Some people who have taken hormones or have had surgeries to aid their transition might prefer the term *transsexual,* but some people find this term offensive and something mostly used by the medical community. The word a person uses to describe his or her gender identity can be a very personal affair, and it is not necessarily linked to any medical procedure.

THE DEAL WITH DOUBLE-DATING

If you are straight, or in a straight relationship, and you decide you want to experiment with bisexuality, don't assume that just because it's with someone of the same gender it will be OK with your partner for you to stray. Unless your boyfriend or girlfriend gives you explicit permission to experiment outside the relationship, it is considered cheating, no matter who it's with.

It's not like it's OK if you are dating a blonde and have sex with a redhead behind the blonde's back, right? Same thing. There is no blurry line here. So if you are even thinking of becoming sexual with anyone else (even just to experiment), you need to talk to the person you are dating.

PHYSICALLY CHANGING GENDERS

So how does one change gender? Some people who question their gender start off dressing in the clothes of the opposite sex, usually in the confines of their bedroom, to see what it feels and looks like. Then, they may start dressing that way out in the world, and may also change their hair, take on a new name, and use the pronoun (he or she) of the new gender. After living as the opposite gender for a period of time, the next step might be to undergo a more physical transition. This is a fairly complex process, which involves talking with a therapist for some time to make sure it's the right decision. It may then involve hormone therapy, or surgery, or both. Each person must decide what is right physically and financially (not all transfolks can afford expensive surgeries) at the given time.

It can be rough for people who are transgender, and there is typically a period of time in which they struggle to figure out if something is wrong with them. There are no specific rules for what to do if you identify as the opposite sex. Some people hide their desire to be the opposite sex. This is like being gay and being in the closet, only the closet is full of someone else's clothes. It sucks because you can't live your life the way you feel most comfortable (dressing and living as someone of the other gender) out of fear of people judging you or being jerks about it. The hope is that, with the love and support of friends and family, a transgender person will be encouraged to live as the gender he or she most identifies with.

SEXUAL REASSIGNMENT SURGERY

If you are thinking about gender reassignment surgery, you'll want to speak to a professional qualified to answer all of your questions. You'll also want to speak with a qualified and trustworthy therapist who specializes in transgender patients. Surgery is a very big step, and you'll need someone there who understands what you are going through.

Here are the basics of how a sex change unfolds. If a female becomes a male, the first surgery is usually to remove the breasts, and the chest comes to look like a male chest. The doctor will then prescribe testosterone to start to enlarge the clitoris, making it look more like a small penis. From there, if genital surgery is desired, the doctor will use the tissue of the enlarged clitoris to form a penis. This surgery is far from perfect, and the new penis will not look exactly like a biological penis, but science is working on this, and it's expected that the procedure will improve in coming years.

For a male who is becoming female, the patient will start taking hormones to help create breasts and may also get breast implants. To create a va-

PRONOUNS

You probably learned a lot about pronouns in grade school, but you probably don't remember too much discussion about gender-neutral pronouns. Now that we're at the brink of a time when people are talking about gender identity openly, it's important that we understand that things aren't as simple as "he" "she" or even "they" anymore. So, what's the right thing to say when referring to someone? If you have your own preference, it would be best for you to just tell people, even though you may feel like you have to repeat yourself a lot. Please be patient. And if you are friends with someone who identifies as trans or queer, go ahead and ask that person directly.

WHAT'S A TRANSVESTITE?

More commonly known as a cross-dresser, this is someone who likes to dress in the clothing of the opposite sex. Cross-dressing does not imply that one is gay or transgender. In fact, 87 percent of cross-dressers are straight! Some guys simply like playing dress-up and role-playing as women (sometimes as a sexual fetish), or just like the feeling and styles of women's clothing. The same goes for women who dress in men's clothing. There are also people who dress up in the clothing of the opposite sex for entertainment purposes, and they are called drag queens (men who dress as women) and drag kings (women who dress as men).

gina, the doctor uses the skin of the penis to form the labia and vaginal walls.

Because the surgery involves creating a vaginal cavity, postoperative women will need to insert into the newly formed vagina an object that is shaped kind of like a dildo (a fake penis, see page 86-87) to make sure everything heals nicely.

Both males and females who have had such surgeries are able to have complete sex lives, including full sensation and orgasm in their new genitals.

GETTING BOXED AND MISLABELED

With all of this orienting and identifying, it's easy for people to get a little label crazy. Labels can be a little annoying when they are the right labels (like being called Shortie when you're short, or Tubby if you're a little chubby), but they can be infuriating when they are wrong (you're straight and everyone is calling you gay or vice versa). That being said, people love to label. They think if they can figure out who you are, they have a better shot at figuring out who they are (not always the case).

Everyone seems to have that one friend that everyone thinks is gay and just in the closet. That friend can swear on a stack of *Playboy* magazines that he's not gay, but his friends won't relent. They say things like, "He's never had a girlfriend" and "He really likes dancing to Madonna while decorating his bedroom." Although those things may be true, they don't mean that he's gay. The same can happen for young girls who are called lesbians simply because they like masculine activities. And just because a guy is really into playing sports or a girl likes makeup, doesn't mean that either of them are necessarily straight.

Society likes to put us into boxes, but guess what? Rainbows, rugby, and mullets don't make a person gay, straight, or transgender. (FYI: Mullets are a bad idea. Period.) Do yourself a huge favor by caring less about what society tells you to think and more about important things, like who you really are… and which celebrities are the hottest.

QUEER BASHING

As nice as it would be for a "queer bash" to be a posh party for homosexual or transgenders, the actual definition isn't as pleasant. Queer bashing is when people verbally and physically abuse others who are (or are thought to be) lesbian, gay, bisexual, or transgender. It can range from name-calling to really nasty violence. Gay boys and girls get called everything from "homo" and "lesbo" to "fag," and they're often told they're disgusting or that God hates them. Sometimes even parents (who should really know better) are involved in this hate-mongering.

When someone is harassed or abused because of their sexual orientation or gender identification, it is considered a hate crime. After the brutal murder of gay Wyoming college student Matthew Shepard, many states passed strict legislation, with severe penalties, against these types of crimes — but they continue to happen on a regular basis. Sexual orientation or gender identity doesn't make a person good or bad. If part of being LGBT was drowning kittens, then it would be a different story. But it's not. In fact, lots of LGBT people love kittens.

So do yourself and humanity a favor — stand up against queer bashing whenever you see it going down. And then get a kitten.

IN THE CLOSET

You've probably heard this phrase, which is used to describe people who have not gone public with their sexual orientation. This phrase is an adaptation of "skeletons in the closet" — which means having something shameful in your life that you need to hide. The use of the phrase in association with people who are not openly gay became popular after World War II, when Americans started fearing that homosexuals (and communists) were going to destroy life as we knew it. Gay people during this time were suddenly getting arrested and being prevented from doing basic things — like working. So, they had to stay "in the closet" about their sexuality. This may explain why houses built during that time have so much extra closet space.

WHAT MEANS WHAT

Here is a short list of the most common sexual orientations and gender identifications.

SEXUAL ORIENTATIONS

- **Heterosexual:** People who are attracted to the opposite gender.
- **Homosexual:** Women who are attracted to other women (lesbians) and men who are attracted to other men (gay). The term *gay* sometimes also refers to lesbians, as well.
- **Bisexual:** People who are attracted to both genders.
- **Pansexuals (aka omnisexuals):** People who are attracted to everyone. This differs from bisexuality only in that the pansexual does not make a distinction between genders and is attracted to people who also do not identify as either gender. (Despite the name, they are not sexually attracted to skillets.)
- **Asexuals:** Unlike pansexuals, asexuals have no sexual desire for anyone. They often have relationships with others who are also asexual, choosing to marry or live together happily without ever having sex.

GENDER IDENTIFICATIONS

• **Cisgender:** People who are comfortable in the gender they were assigned at birth.

• **Transgender:** People who feel there is a difference between their birth gender and the gender they truly are. This usually includes transsexuals, some asexuals, and gender-queers. Many transgender people identify simply as trans.

• **Transsexual:** People who feel that they were born as the wrong gender and choose to live as the other gender. Many will also identify as trans, transgender, or as the gender they are living as.

• **Intersexual:** Anyone born with atypical sex chromosomes and/or sexual anatomy that doesn't fall under what we consider standard female or male. For example, an intersex person may look female on the outside but have male genitalia, or vice versa, or an intersex person's genitalia may look like something in between a penis and a vagina.

• **Genderqueer:** People who don't identify with their given gender but don't want to transition to the opposite gender. They reject traditional ideas of gender, feeling that no single label can express their gender experience. Genderqueers can feel they are neither male nor female, both male and female, or somewhere in between. They are often categorized as third gender, bi-gender, multi-gender, and gender benders.

WHAT NOW?

Now you probably have more info than you know what to do with. Perhaps you feel overwhelmed thinking you have to choose a label for yourself. Or maybe you know who you are and are simply glad to learn about who else is out there. Either scenario is perfectly acceptable, but, if you're all confused now and freaking out about your sexual orientation or gender identity, calm down for a second and remember: You can take as long as you like on this one — there is nobody standing in line behind you, waiting for you to figure it out. •

Q & A

Q. My best friend has been acting really weird lately. We had a sleepover a few weeks ago, and we were just playing around and a song came on about girls kissing each other, so we kissed. I laughed about it, but she seemed upset after. Now she avoids me at school but won't stop text messaging me after saying that we really need to talk. I keep telling her that if she wants to talk she should stop ditching me at school, but she does it anyway. I'm not stupid. I know she probably has a crush on me or something. I just don't know why she's acting mean to me, then trying to talk to me when nobody else is around. What should I tell her?

A. *It's hard to know exactly what she's thinking without asking her, but your friend probably had some feelings about that kiss that are confusing her now. What you need to find out from her is if those feelings are the good kind or the icky kind. She may be worried that you have a crush on her and that if she's nice to you she'll be leading you on. She may have a crush on you. Or maybe she's just worried that your friendship won't be* the same anymore because of one kiss. This happens all the time in the movies, but in those cases it's all wrapped up nicely in 90 minutes.

The easiest thing you could do is to meet up with her after school so that she can talk to you. It's pretty useless to sit around and wonder what is going on when she is giving you an option to ask her face-to-face. Before you talk to her, consider all of the different things she may say to you and figure out how you feel about them. If you were close enough friends that you could get all kissy-faced before, you should be able to talk things through now.

Q. My dad was straight when he was with my mom, but he came out when they broke up. A year later he was straight again, so is he gay or straight?

A. Sexuality isn't always as simple as gay or straight. Because of that, some people go through life going back and forth. The most likely explanation for your father's choices is that he is bisexual. With time, he may pick a team to hit for, or he may just keep flip-flopping, but for now it seems that you're accepting of his shifting sexuality, and that's the most important thing. Hopefully, he'll also be understanding and patient when you are trying to figure things out in your life.

Q. My brother and I go to school with this kid, and everyone knows he's gay. He makes fun of everybody, and we can't stand him. My mom says that we have to be nice to him, because being mean to gay people is wrong. Why do gay people have to be such jerks?

A. We know plenty of straight people who are jerks as well, so let's be clear: Being a jerk is a universal trait that defies sexual orientation. This guy might be hard to put up with, but it's not because of his sexuality, and even if he's irritable and defensive because of all of the teasing he has to put up with (you'd probably be irritable and defensive, too, if everyone was always on your case), that doesn't give him the right to be a jerk. Short people have to put up with a lot of teasing, and they don't get the luxury of being rude.

This guy would probably be nicer to you if you were nicer to him. If you want to test out the theory, try it for a few days and see if his tune changes. If he's still a jerk to you, at least you might stop thinking of him as a gay jerk and merely as a jerk. With your new open mind, the next gay guy at school might become your best friend.

Q. I'm a gay 16-year-old guy, and I've been out for about a year, but my family doesn't know. I've had the same boyfriend for nine months, but my parents think he's my friend and I'm afraid that if I tell them, they won't let us hang out anymore. I also have no idea how to tell them I'm gay. What should I do?

A. Hearing that a son or daughter is gay or a lesbian (or transgender, for that matter) isn't a big deal for some parents but can be shocking for others. It can trigger a lot of different emotions. If there is a bit of freaking out at first, hopefully your parents — after the shock wears off — will accept you for who you are. (Your boyfriend may not be invited to stay for sleepovers right away, but neither would your girlfriend if you were straight.) With a little time (and a lot of good talks), things will probably get back to normal. If you're worried about coming out, forge ahead with a plan to tell one relative at a time. You might think announcing it to the whole family at once, like at Thanksgiving dinner, would be a good idea, but think again.

Of course, there are exceptions. Some families turn ugly when they hear the news, going so far as to kick a son or daughter out of the house, send a child to a special camp with the intent to un-gay him or her, or be physically or verbally abusive. If you think any of this is possible, recon-

sider coming out to your parents while you are still living at home. If you do decide to open up to them, make sure you have some support to cope with the backlash. This could be an LGBT rights group in your area (see resources on pages 184-185) or a supportive adult who could step in if the situation were to become dangerous.

Q. I am a girl, but I love to play soccer, lift weights, and work on my car on the weekends. Do you think I might be trans?

A. Just because you are a girl who likes to kick butt in soccer (or a guy who likes to wear dresses to costume parties) does not mean you are trans. The real tip-off that you may be trans is the desire to live your life with a different outward gender identity than the one you were given at birth. So if you're a little bit of a tomboy or a girlie man, there's no need to book gender-reassignment surgery just yet.

THERE ARE NO STUPID QUESTIONS — EXCEPT FOR THIS ONE

Q. It seems like all the gay dudes at my school hang out with the hot chicks. Should I go gay for a while just to get some action?

CHAPTER 3

MASTURBATION

The Greatest Love of All

Now that you're a little more in touch with your body, let's talk about actually touching your body. Hello, masturbation. As you may know, masturbation is touching yourself in a sexual way that causes arousal. It can be done with special toys or simply with your hand. It's like having your very own party for yourself — only you don't have to worry about what to wear or send out an invitation. It's also one of the cheapest, safest, and most effective stress relievers for a teen.

If you're thinking about having sex, masturbating is an excellent way to prepare. Great sex is all about communication, and you can't tell a partner that what's being done is wrong or right if you don't know what right is to you. So, before you drop your pants for your gf or bf, get to know what your body likes.

WHO MASTURBATES?

Odds are, you and your friends talk about sex a lot more than you talk about masturbation (unless you are calling each other names in the cafeteria). There are a couple of reasons why some people get freaked about the subject. For one, medical doctors used to argue that it was unhealthy. In fact, it was often called "self-pollution" in the 1830s and through the early 1900s. In the 1960s, the medical community finally agreed that it was natural and healthy, but masturbation's reputation never really recovered. People still think of it as something that only losers do.

Movies don't help this idea much. If a mainstream movie features a masturbating kid, it is always the total dork or freak doing it and everyone finds out and makes a big joke out of it. No wonder your friends would rather admit to watching a public television marathon than touching themselves. The truth is, most people masturbate. It would be nice if there were numbers and math-related things that could be turned into graphs that a guy with a pointer could show us to illustrate just how many people masturbate, and how many do not. But, unfortunately, there is no conclusive study on this. *The Kinsey Report*, which was written

back when your grandparents were masturbating but gets updated from time to time, says that 98 percent of undergraduate college men and 44 percent of undergraduate college women had reported rubbing one out. Since then, thousands of other scientists have wasted valuable masturbation time trying to come up with a more accurate number.

WHERE, WHEN, WHY, AND HOW

If you haven't started masturbating yet, or even if you have, you may have some very basic questions about it.

WHERE?

While masturbation is normal, it is meant to be done in private. Public masturbation is a sure way to get your picture on the local sex offender site — which is more exclusive than some social networks, but less likely to land you any dates. Traditional and safe areas for masturbating include your bedroom or bathroom. Wherever it is, make sure it's private and you can lock the door.

The bathtub or shower is a great environment to get it on with yourself. You're already naked, and cleanup is minimal. You may be inclined to reach for shampoo or conditioner to provide lubrication for the act, but beware that lots of these products can cause the sensitive skin on your sensitive parts to become irritated faster than you can climax. Even soap can be irritating. When possible, use spit or water-based lubricants, and opt for things that are fragrance-free.

WHEN?

Whenever you feel like it, so long as you're in a private place and not putting off your homework, of course.

WHY?

You don't really need a reason. Some people masturbate when they think about that hottie down the block, or that anchor on the local evening newscast, and others simply masturbate to pass the time when they are bored.

HOW?

Luckily, you only have yourself to impress, so this isn't going to be as difficult as you think (unless you are the type who has ridiculously high standards).

Masturbation is about self-exploration, so feel free to poke, stroke, tap, and wiggle in whatever ways you would like until you discover what feels the best to you. You might find one particular way of doing it that feels the best and stick with it, or you may decide to switch things up just to keep things fresh. The only real rule is: Do whatever feels good.

Tips for Girls. The first step is to locate your clitoris. The clitoris is a bundle of thousands of nerves packaged in a pea-sized (more or less) knob, located just north of your urethra (where the pee comes out). For a diagram of where it's located, refer back to page 10. The clitoris is unlike any other part of the male or female body in that it has only one job: to enhance sexual pleasure. It's like having an assistant whose only worry is to make you feel great whenever you pay attention to her. There are a lot

YOU NAME IT

There are lots of different words for masturbation. Here are some of our faves: badgering the witness, beating your meat, double clicking the mouse, fluffin' the muffin, jacking off, polishing the silver, rubbing one out, spanking the monkey, tickling the taco, waxing the bishop.

SEXY TIME IN YOUR DREAMS

Once upon a time, young people were told that having "nocturnal emissions" (or sexual dreams that result in having an orgasm) would cause them to go crazy or get flesh-eating diseases. This resulted in much panic because most people have no control over their dreams and having wet dreams is a natural part of developing. Good news: It turns out that you won't lose your mind from having an orgasm in your sleep! While both guys and girls can have dreams about sex, only guys will have a mess to clean up. In fact, the only negative thing about wet dreams is that they create more laundry for guys. Do your parents a huge favor and start washing your own clothes and sheets. It's about time you did that anyway.

of jokes about how hard it can be to find the clit (as it's often nicknamed), so some girls are surprised at just how obvious it is. For other girls it can take some searching, especially if they're trying to find it when they are not turned on.

Like the penis, the clit fills up with blood when you start to get revved up, so if you are trying to find it for the first time and you already know what gets you in the mood, get excited, then start to feel around.

Once you find your clitoris, you can touch it in a bunch of different ways, trying a variety of pressures and speeds, to see what feels right. You may want to use lubrication. Some people also use various kinds of sex toys like dildos and vibrators (see pages 86-87 for more on what these are), or masturbate in the shower, using the water pressure from a showerhead. As you masturbate and it feels good, you may get increasingly more excited. Your body may start to tense up and feel good, and you may have an orgasm. An orgasm is when your body parts are stimulated in such a way that the muscles in your sexual organs involuntarily spasm. It usually feels really good.

Don't get frustrated if you figure out what you like and it doesn't work the same the next time. You don't wear the same outfit or eat the same lunch every day. Why should you have to masturbate the same way every time?

Some girls who masturbate a lot or get used to high pressure toys find that they can't orgasm without really rubbing hard and for a long time. Luckily, you can't break your clitoris, but if you've reached a place where your hand can't keep up with what your body needs, ease up for a while. Use a very light touch and focus more on the whole process instead of the end result.

Techniques for the Gents. Stroke it, yank it, pull it, rub it: Really, anything goes. You can also rub your penis on a mattress, between two pillows, or on a piece of clothing. However, do not use your mother's cashmere sweater. No matter how soft and luscious it feels, the dry cleaners and your family will find the fallout from the deed hard to forgive. While masturbating, your penis will become erect and after some time, you may have an orgasm and ejaculate semen. (If you ejaculate something else, like gold coins or html code, seek medical attention.)

You can encircle your whole fist around the shaft, use only your index finger and thumb for a more delicate touch, or reverse your grip for a backhanded rubdown. To spice things up, use your less dexterous hand to provide a different sensation. This is sometimes called "old lefty," but in areas of Wisconsin it's more popularly titled "milking betsy after sunset." Though creativity is encouraged, so is caution. Some guys try using different tools, but that can cause trouble, specifically citrus fruits because they can burn you outside and inside.

BEWARE OF THE DEATH GRIP!

This is a common mistake made by boys who apply a little too much pressure during their alone-time adventures. Unfortunately, by the time these boys become sexually active, their penises have become accustomed to a rigorous style of jerking that most partners will find difficult to match. Thus, they cannot reach climax or even sexual arousal unless their penis is stuck in a vice grip jacking it at 100 mph. Sure, there will be those instances when one is short on time and only the death grip will do. But be sure to mix it up and introduce your penis to more delicate and gentle sensations.

MASTURBATION FANTASIES

Sometimes people fantasize when they masturbate, and the things people fantasize about are often nothing like reality. You might think about the Phantom of the Opera kidnapping you and doing naughty things to you in his lair. Or you might think about food when you get really worked up. But that doesn't mean that if the real Phantom of the Opera kidnapped you, you'd be too happy about it, and in real life you probably don't want to take a chicken pot pie on a date. Point is, don't get too upset if you are thinking about things that seem extra naughty or just plain weird while you masturbate.

WHAT IS AN ORGASM?

An orgasm is what happens when, during sexual activity, your body parts are stimulated in the right way, and the muscles in your sexual organs involuntarily spasm in rapid, rhythmic contractions. Your brain also releases endorphins causing a sudden feeling of euphoria. Other parts of your body may shake, quiver, or spasm during an orgasm, too. The penis will usually release cum, and, for some women, the vagina will also release fluid. For most people, an orgasm feels really good and even like a "release" of tension in the body. Kind of like a sneeze. But better. An orgasm can occur during masturbation, foreplay, or sex. •

Q & A

Q. Am I masturbating too much?

A. *That depends. Have you masturbated four times since you started this chapter? Well, even if the answer is yes, it's not necessarily a problem. As long as masturbating isn't getting in the way of your daily responsibilities, you're fine. And if you make it one of your daily responsibilities, that's fine, too.*

Q. Is it normal to masturbate if I have a partner with whom I am sexually active?

A. *Definitely. Masturbation is way different from partnered sex. Having regular booty doesn't necessarily decrease the desire for masturbation. Sex and masturbation don't feel the same to your body or your brain. During sex you will find that your focus is also on the other person, so you don't have the freedom to just wander off in thought or get things done quick and easy if you feel like it. With masturbation, you are the only person that matters, and that is a nice option.*

Q. I haven't masturbated yet, and my closest friends say that they do it all the time. Is there something wrong with me?

A. *Don't worry. This doesn't mean you are destined to be a circus side-show act. There are a couple of reasons you may not be into it. For one, you might be shy about your body or feel disconnected from it. If you have always been told, as most people have, that you need to cover your body because those are your private parts, you may have gotten the idea that those parts are so private that you shouldn't even try poking at them. Getting comfortable with your body can take some time.*

But it's also important to remember that we all have different sexual needs and interest levels through our entire lives. Some people never masturbate at all, some people start when they are really young, and some people get around to it later. Do what feels right to you, and don't compare yourself with other people.

Q. I have been masturbating for almost six years and I am getting bored with just regular masturbation. Is there anything I can do to keep it interesting?

A. *You could try playing video games while masturbating. Or perhaps you could take up skydiving and masturbate while jumping out of a plane. That could get expensive, though. But seriously, this is a great question because it is kind of like you are in a long-term relationship with your hand and somewhere along the way things got old. So, what can you do to spice up your masturbation life?*

You could try anal play (playing with your butt while you get off). Also, as with partner sex, changing the positions and switching to different locations (private locations!) helps. Use your imagination to fantasize and try different textures, such as putting on a condom with some lubricant inside. Trying new things is important in everything you do, and this is no exception. But remember: You don't want to do anything that might hurt your body. You can permanently injure yourself if you don't know what you're doing or shove things into places they don't belong.

Q. What's the difference between a dildo and a vibrator? They look like the same thing.

A. A dildo is a penis-shaped sex toy meant for insertion into the butt or the vagina. (It's also an insult that teenage boys like to lob at each other.) For people who enjoy penetration, this is the sex toy for them. A vibrator is any sex toy that hums, shakes, and buzzes when you use it. It typically requires batteries. Sometimes vibrators are dildos as well (yay for innovation). Vibrators are great for stimulating the clitoris, the penis, or the testicles.

Q. I don't orgasm when I masturbate. Is there something wrong with me?

A. Masturbation doesn't have to lead to orgasm. If you are enjoying the sensation of touching yourself much more than the end result, you can use that time to explore your body and not worry about the not-so-grand finale. That said, if you are finding that your orgasms are not producing the awe-inspiring high you've heard about from others, the problem is either mental or physical, or a combination of the two.

If it's mental, it's important to understand why. Anxiety is a total mood killer, and if you worry too much about having an orgasm, it is totally possible to psych yourself out of it. Of course, now you may become anxious about being anxious. Please don't do that. Instead, try some breathing techniques and aromatherapy, and calm the heck down before you get yourself worked up.

If it's physical, it's usually something that can change. For instance, things like lack of exercise, poor health in general, drinking, and drug use (legal or illegal) can all have an effect on your sexual performance.

As the years go by and your body goes through changes, you may find that the sensation of your orgasms changes. Just because you aren't having the best sex with yourself this year, that doesn't mean that you won't hit your stride later on.

Q. Can I masturbate with my boyfriend or girlfriend?

A. Oh, yes. Mutual masturbation — which may sound like an investment term, but really just means masturbating in front of each other — is common and is a way for you to see what your boy or girlfriend likes instead of making you guess. And it's the safest sex there is!

THERE ARE NO STUPID QUESTIONS — EXCEPT FOR THIS ONE

Q. Can I get my mom pregnant if I masturbate in a sock and then my mom washes the dirty sock, gets dried semen on her hand, and later wipes herself?

CHAPTER 4

THE FIRST TIME

What to Know, What to Expect

You've got a lot of choices to make as you get older, like what to study in school, or whether you're going to shave off your eyebrows before picture day. One of the many (and one of the most important) choices you have to make is if you are ready to have sex — or to take part in any sexual activity. How will you know when it is time? Is there some sort of checklist you can refer to? A handy quiz you can take?

Not really. The best way to decide if you are ready is to make sure you have all the facts, evaluate the pros and cons, and go with how you feel. And keep in mind that each time you get physical with someone new, you have to think about this stuff all over again. Some guidance is always helpful, so here are a few basic things you should know about and consider.

WHAT IS VIRGINITY?

If you're gonna "give it up," you might want to know what that means. For a long time, society defined "sex" as the penetration of the vagina by the penis, and so that was the only way to lose one's virginity. But that's not the case these days. Sex is looked at in a broader context, and not just in terms of traditional heterosexual-style sex. And that means there are many ways to lose one's virginity.

For lesbians, partaking in oral sex or fingering would totally count as losing their virginity. For gay males it may be oral or anal sex, giving or receiving. For straight kids, it may be the ol' penis in the vagina but could also be any of the above. (More about all of these in the next chapter.) The point is, don't go around claiming to be a virgin just because you're only doing anal.

Of course, you may find yourself ready for one type of sex before another, and that's perfectly fine. Do only what is most comfortable and safest for you.

HOW TO DECIDE IF THE TIME IS RIGHT

People decide to have sex for the first time for a lot of different reasons. Often, they are in a relationship and the choice is based on affection or love. Other times, it's based purely on lust. And sometimes people decide to do it because they feel pressured, or simply think it's about time to get it done, as if it is a task on a checklist.

Before having sex for the first time, or any time, consider the following:

- Are you doing it because you want to do it or because someone else wants you to (or because you feel like you should just get it over with already)? If you're not doing it because you want to, you shouldn't be doing it at all.
- Do you know all of the risks of sex, and how to best prevent pregnancy and disease (see Chapters 7 and 8)? If you don't have a really, really good understanding of all of this, you are not ready to have sex.

- What are your own personal beliefs about sex? Do you think it's OK to do it before you get married? Do you think it's OK to do it with someone you may not love? You need to make these decisions for yourself and be sure about them. There are no right or wrong answers, but if you end up doing something that you don't feel 100 percent about, you may end up with feelings of guilt or regret, and that isn't fun for anyone. Most likely, your first time will not be exactly what you imagined, but it shouldn't totally suck or be something that makes you feel bad about yourself.

- Do you think it will make you either more or less complete than you already are? If so, you should wait a bit longer. Having sex does not, and should not, change who you are as a person or how you feel about yourself.

- Are you doing it to try to get something from someone (attention, love, money) or to seek revenge on someone? If so, you should remember that using sex as a tool for reward or punishment is never effective in the long term and will leave you feeling worse than you did before.

The bottom line is that when you choose to have sex, you should be doing it because you want to, not because you were pressured by friends or by a partner. Think about how very hot it is when someone has the courage of his or her conviction. Your story about choosing to stay a virgin won't be made into a major motion picture, but your choice is still important and empowering.

KNOWING THE RISKS INVOLVED

Making the decision to have sex for the first time is a big deal for everyone, but it often feels bigger for girls. There are good reasons for that. If you are a straight girl having intercourse, you're at risk of getting pregnant, you're at a higher risk than straight boys of contracting disease, and, well, it can hurt. That last one is also true for lesbian girls. These are not reasons not to do it, but they are reasons to think carefully before you do it.

If you're a straight guy, you should still be concerned about getting the girl pregnant (after all, that whole process would involve you), and all guys are also at risk for picking up a disease.

Be smart about taking this leap and learn about what's involved and how to protect yourself. Read Chapters 7 and 8 to learn more about how to prevent pregnancy and sexually transmittable infections and diseases. And always use a condom.

CONSENT

Before anything at all happens, make sure that you have a good understanding of what "consent" means. This is serious stuff, so pay attention. (You know, in case you were trying to read this while watching TV and taking a nap...)

Consenting to any sexual act is extremely important on the parts of all people involved. It doesn't matter which gender you are, even if you've said yes already, or even if you've had sex with the person on previous occasions. You (and the person you're getting busy with) have the right to stop, just as you have the right not to start in the first place. Saying "no" seems like the easiest thing in the world, right? How many times have you said it to a parent or teacher? How many times has it been said to you? But often when it comes to sex, saying "no" or "stop" is difficult, especially if you think the other person is going to be really upset with you.

Also, when your blood isn't exactly providing any help to your brains because you're all worked up, hearing "no" might lead you to act more aggressively than you should. However, stopping things right away is a lot

LOSING IT

The slang out there describing losing your virginity are generally negative, especially for girls. You either "lost it," "gave it away," or were "deflowered." Great. But remember that those are just old-fashioned expressions that came to be during a time when sex was a very taboo subject and people believed, out of ignorance, that if a woman had sex she lost her innocence or integrity. Now we know that having sex does not mean you "lose" anything (or "take" anything from another person), or that you become a less valuable person.

better in the long run.

That's why you should always have sex with people you feel comfortable talking to, always stay in communication throughout, and know yourself enough to be able to confidently speak up if you're uncomfortable.

In short, no means no, it's okay to say no, and don't start having sex until you already know how to say no.

DON'T BE JAILBAIT

Each state has different laws regarding sex, including the age you must be to have sex and the acceptable age difference between you and the person you are having sex with. Some states have different laws for homosexual sex. Some states have two ages of consent: One is the age you can have sex if your parents give you permission, and the other is the age at which you no longer need your parents to give you the thumbs-up. If it sounds confusing, that's because it is. You may think you are ready at 14 to have sex with your 18-year-old boyfriend or girlfriend, but, depending on where you live (and who finds out about it), it could land one of you in the slammer. Sex is great, but it's not worth a prison term or stint in juvenile hall.

Because the laws can change, search out a reliable and frequently updated source from which you can learn your own state's laws. (Your friend's mom's hairstylist doesn't count as a reliable source, and neither do daytime talk show hosts.) Use a trusted government website to make sure you have the correct information.

By the way, law enforcement officials in some states attempt to uphold old laws that made it illegal to have oral and anal sex. If you live in one of those states and disagree with the way the law is being interpreted, find a local LGBT (lesbian gay bisexual transgender) rights group or contact the American Civil Liberties Union (ACLU) and find a nonviolent way to work together and get your voices heard.

GETTING NAKED!

Does the thought of all those dangling body parts (your own and your partner's) gross you out? You may want to get more comfortable with your body (and your partner's) if you are swapping an all-access pass.

To get to know your own body, spend some good solid time looking in the mirror, exploring things, and checking out what each part does. (Masturbation is a great help here — read Chapter 3 to get a better handle on it.) Make sure you also feel ready to get cozy with your partner's entryways and appendages. If you want to put part of yourself inside a vagina, you shouldn't think of it as nasty. If you are interested in getting personal

DON'T BE A SACK RACER!

If you're getting hot and heavy with your special someone and you haven't yet considered if you are ready to have sex (with that particular person, or at all), this is the wrong time to make the choice. When you're in the midst of a hot make-out session, all of the blood your brain usually uses to make decisions is busy filling up other parts of your body. That means you're not thinking straight. So, even though things may feel right at that moment, you could wind up making a decision that you'll regret. You will have other opportunities to get it on, so there's no need to rush into things.

with a penis, you should understand how it works and feel comfortable touching it.

WILL IT HURT?

A lot of straight girls, as well as lesbians who are engaging in some kind of penetration, are worried that sex will hurt the first time, or that they will bleed. The answer to both is that it might. It's different for everyone. Most females are born with a hymen, which is a thin piece of skinlike tissue at the opening of the vagina, but sometimes there's so little tissue it might seem like there's no hymen. When you have sex for the first time, the hymen may tear and there may be some blood. (You may have heard a story about how, back in the day, women's sheets were checked for blood after their wedding night to be sure that the woman was a virgin when she got married.) This is why losing one's virginity is sometimes known as "popping the cherry."

However, for most girls, the hymen tears before they ever have sex, from stretching, athletics, horseback riding, masturbating, or inserting a tampon. New research even says that, as estrogen levels rise in your body, your hymen starts to wear away naturally. And some girls have super-stretchy hymens that never actually "break." Even if your hymen does tear during the first time, a number of women find that there is little or no bleeding involved. In situations where there is, it isn't a gushing river of blood.

A LOT OF CHICKENS LOST THEIR LIVES

In Sudan, it was customary for a newly married couple to hang their bedsheets on a clothes line for the villagers and in-laws to see the spots of blood that would prove that the bride was pure. Because women don't always bleed their first time, families would resort to using animal blood, which they would place in a small pouch made of animal intestines and insert into the bride's vagina. Yeah, gross.

As for pain during their first time, girls report varying degrees. It will actually be more uncomfortable if you are scared and not relaxed because the vaginal muscles will be too tense and tight to allow the penis (or even fingers) to pass through the opening. So, if you have made the decision to have sex, try to relax, as that will make it more comfortable for you.

So just take it slow and gentle, and keep communicating with your partner. If there is a lot of pain at any time, stop and try again another day. If you experience pain every time you have sex, definitely check in with your gynecologist (and you should have one if you are sexually active) to see what's up.

PERFORMANCE ANXIETY

It's perfectly normal to feel nervous about your first time. Having sex is completely different from masturbating, and you have no way of really knowing what it is going to feel like. For girls, being anxious or tense can make getting anything inside there more difficult (as mentioned above). For guys, the excitement and anxiety of having sex for the first time can cause problems like premature ejaculation, which is just a fancy term for having an orgasm really quickly. You may also find that your head on your shoulders is messing with the head in your trousers and suddenly you have trouble getting a boner (ironic considering it usually happens so easily and at the most inopportune times). Despite all of the advertisements you have seen for pills that make you last longer or get hard, you don't need to seek the assistance of modern medicine to make sure you are a total stud your first time.

As cheesy as it sounds, if you really get to know your partner before having sex, both of you will feel much more at ease if you have to deal with any issue that arises — or doesn't. If anything is not working the way it seems it should, take a deep breath and talk to your partner about it. Don't sweat it if it doesn't happen this time — it certainly won't be your last chance.

THE COMEDY OF SEX

As much as sex can be a beautiful, wonderful, hot, sweaty lovefest, it can also be awkward — especially the first time (or even the first few times), or the first time with a new partner. Both people involved are anxious and unaccustomed to each other's bodies, and all sorts of funny things can happen. Your body will make sounds, start to smell different, and excrete various fluids. Things will be slippery, and they won't always do exactly what you want them to. If you take a lighthearted approach and have a sense of humor about it all, it will make it much easier for you to laugh and not stress when weird farty noises or seemingly involuntary body movements occur.

WILL I HAVE AN ORGASM?

As mentioned in Chapter 3, an orgasm is what happens when, during sexual activity, your body parts are stimulated in the right way, and the muscles in your sexual organs involuntarily spasm in rapid, rhythmic contractions. It usually feels good, like a deep release of built-up tension. Orgasms also release endorphins, which are the body's natural stress relievers, into the bloodstream. (Exercise and laughter do the same thing but are not always as much fun.)

Some guys orgasm right away if it's their first time, while others find that they just keep going well beyond the time that their partner is still enjoying things. You can use masturbation as an exercise to train your brain and your penis. You can use certain images, as well as certain types of pressures and strokes, to help along or restrain an orgasm. You can even practice "edging," which is when you get yourself right to the point when you are about to cum, then you stop or slow down. And for girls, well, you may or may not orgasm the first time. You may also find that you can orgasm more easily from foreplay (see Chapter 5) or oral sex (see Chapter 6) than from vaginal sex. And you could also potentially orgasm before your partner does. So, again, keep communicating, and keep your expectations reasonable. And don't feel bad if your first time is not mind-blowing. If it's nice and respectful and fun, you are way ahead of the game.

TALK TO ME

When you are having sex for the first time, make sure you talk to your partner about what he or she wants and feels before you start doing it. If you are a lesbian, you will need to determine with your girlfriend what it is that you consider having sex. It could be fingering, inserting other objects, rubbing your bodies together, or oral. If you are a gay male, you'll likely also want to talk to your partner about what kind of sex you want to have. Homosexual males can have sex in many ways — such as oral sex or anal sex. They can also reach orgasm through activities like rubbing, mutual masturbation, and hand jobs. When it comes to anal sex, some only give, some only receive, and some forgo anal altogether. If you are a straight couple, you should also consider how far you want to go and what things you might want to do. Don't wait until you get into the heat of the moment before having that talk.

And always check in with your partner during sex to make sure everything is going OK — if they're enjoying it, or if they're in any pain or discomfort. Sex can be awkward, but it should feel good. If what you're doing hurts or is uncomfortable, stop and try doing something else. •

Q & A

Q. I had a boyfriend last year, and we had sex a bunch of times. Will my new boyfriend still want to have sex with me when he finds out that I am all loose and stretched out?

A. *Having sex does not loosen your vagina. That is a myth, and it has led teen boys in locker rooms to make stupid jokes about tight vaginas for decades. Vaginas are closed, or collapsed, muscular canals, and when nothing is in them, the muscular walls rest against themselves. So when you're just doing normal stuff during the day, your vagina is closed, not open. But when you put something inside the vagina — a tampon, a finger — it expands to make room for what's inside of it. This pliability and softness makes it possible for things to go into the vagina and babies to come out of the vagina. And when the object leaves, the muscles collapse again. Some women report that their vaginas feel a bit stretched after giving birth, but your vagina is definitely not "all loose and stretched out" just because you've had sex.*

Q. I was pressured into having sex for my first time, and because of this one time I am no longer a virgin. It seems kind of pointless to not have sex, since I've already lost my virginity. Is it OK to just have sex with any guy who wants me?

A. *Each time you have sex with someone, it is a new choice. You are able to make choices as you go along that are based on your experiences in life. It sounds like your first experience was not a positive one, and that sucks because it can make you feel really down about yourself and about sex. But use your past to learn and help you in the future.*

If you want to have sex again and you feel comfortable with your body and feel like you are comfortable with the person you want to have sex with, go for it. If you are having sex only because you feel like it is all you have to offer, then please take some time to learn to see yourself as an entire person with a lot to offer.

Q. I'm gay, and I love my boyfriend. Pretty much all of my friends are having sex. They all talk about how much they are doing it and how many people they are doing it with. I don't want to have sex yet, and I think that if I do have sex it will just be to shut them up. Should I lie to them to get them off my back? You know, like, tell them I am having sex so they will stop telling me how weird I am?

A. *First and foremost, you should know that not all of your friends are having sex. In fact, according to a recent study, only 32 percent of ninth graders, 44 percent of tenth graders, and 53 percent of eleventh graders are having sex, so odds are a lot of the people who say they're doing it are probably lying. All this is doing is making the problem worse for everyone. It is far more respectable for you to take a stand when it comes to your personal choices regarding sexual readiness. You might even inspire more kids to come forward and talk about their own abstinence.*

That being said, whether or not you are having sex is no one's business but your own. So, you also have every right to tell them that you simply don't want to talk about it.

Q. My mom says that she will be able to tell when I have started having sex. She says that my body will start to change and I will get more curves. I've also heard that I will smell different. I admit that I like the idea of having boobs, because right now I am as flat as a pancake, but it worries me that everyone will know that I am having sex and start to think I am easy. How can I stop my body from changing when I go all the way with my boyfriend?

SNIFF.

A. *In previous generations it was believed that your body started to change when you began having sex, but that is a complete and total myth. Your physical appearance doesn't reveal whether you've lost your virginity. Your body changes on its own as you experience puberty. Even the most chaste of girls cannot stop the flow of nature. And if you were hoping to inspire some boobs to pop up by getting laid, you're flat out of luck on that front, too.*

Q. Being a virgin is really important to me, and I made a promise to my family that I would not have sex before marriage. I am seeing this really cool boy, and we have done some kissing and fooling around. He says that we can have anal sex and I will still be a virgin. Is that true? I don't want him to break up with me if I don't do it, but I want to make sure I'll still be keeping my promise.

A. *Anal sex is sex. Oral sex is sex. You can read more about both in Chapter 6. If the promise you have made to your family is based on moral beliefs that sex is something you save for the person you marry, and if this is something that you believe as well, any kind of sex is just as immoral as another. The risk of infection with anal sex is at least as high as with other forms of sex (see Chapter 7), and the act itself takes a lot of preparation. If this is something you want to do because you feel as though it is right for you, do some research, talk more with your boyfriend, and make that choice together. If you are just doing it to stay a virgin, you are out of luck. As for keeping your boy around, well, if a dude can't find a reason to stay with you beyond letting him stick it in your butt, he isn't worth your time. (Even if he's really cute.)*

Q. What sort of stuff should I keep with me so that when I have my first time it works out well? I don't want it to suck, so I already keep a sexy pair of underwear in my backpack at all times, but there must be some other things that can help.

A. *One really important part of being ready to have sex for the first time is knowing how to have safe sex the first time. This doesn't mean you need to pack a helmet and safety belt, but it does mean you should know about the equivalent of a helmet and safety belt for sex.*

Ladies, you have an easier time of this. Carrying a purse means you have the space for all sorts of items, useless and useful. You should have at least three condoms (seems hopeful, but you'll want backup in case there are any malfunctions, and three is a pretty magic number). Also, consider toting a few small packs of lubrication. Lubrication will make sex easier, especially if it's the first time. Find a water-based, nonscented lube that comes in a small package. (More about this in later chapters.) If you are not currently on a backup form of birth control, like the pill, you may also want to have emergency contraception (like Plan B) around, in case the condom breaks. Read more about disease prevention and birth control in Chapters 7 and 8.

Q. I was raped as a young girl, and because of this I feel like I have lost the magic. Is there any point in trying to have sex again?

A. You call what happened to you "losing the magic," as if a unicorn were stolen from inside you the day your abuser raped you. You are just as magical as ever, if not more so because you are alive and able to talk about what happened to you. Don't screw that up by thinking of yourself as ruined. If one of your close friends came to you and told you she had been raped, would you tell her that there is something wrong with her as a person? Of course not. As hard as it may be, you need to see the rape as something that happened in the past that does not affect who you are today and your worth as a totally desirable sexual being.

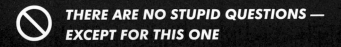

THERE ARE NO STUPID QUESTIONS — EXCEPT FOR THIS ONE

Q. I was having sex with my girlfriend, and we were both virgins, but she didn't bleed. Then we had anal sex and her butt did bleed. Is her hymen in her butt?

CHAPTER 5

FOREPLAY

Getting It On Before Getting It On

Intercourse is usually a hot topic on high school campuses, but there are a lot of other fun ways to get busy before you actually... get busy. That's what foreplay is about — it's the appetizer to the main dish, the previews that set the tone before the epic movie. If you are already having sex with your bf or gf, you can start with other stuff and make the experience less rushed and more significant. And if you are not yet ready to go all the way, there's still a lot of other stuff you can do that's fun and also safer. Foreplay can be enough for some couples and can lead to an orgasm, too.

If you're wondering what actually counts as foreplay, it's typically considered to be anything you do before oral, vaginal, or anal sex. (Anything sexual that is. Taking your shoes off: not foreplay.) Whether you're making out, feeling each other up, or exploring each other's genitals with your hands, these things can all be considered foreplay.

GOOD PREPARATION

Foreplay is a good way to prepare for sex because it gets the body's sexual juices flowing. When you start fooling around, both of you will experience increased blood flow to your genitals, meaning a guy will get an erection, and a girl's clitoris will engorge (a fancy way of saying it gets a little stiffer and bigger). The vagina will also dilate, which means there's more space to store a penis in it for a little while, and it will start to lubricate itself, which is always handy when something's going to be put inside it.

KISSING

Kissing can make a lot of people nervous because no one wants to forever be labeled a bad kisser. It would be awesome if there were no such thing as a bad kisser, but there is. A good kisser pays attention to how the person he or she is kissing is reacting. A great kiss is a real turn-on, so if you're diving in and the person is leaning into you and seems short of breath, and you can feel his or her pulse quicken, you're doing something right. Start slow, and if, as you get more into it, you sense that your kissing partner isn't really into those tongue swirlies you're doing, ease off a bit and try new things until you get the formula right.

Everyone has a different idea of the perfect kiss, therefore how you kiss one person could be drastically different from how you kiss someone else. So, as you're getting to know someone, it's best to be patient and tune in to your partner. Rather than launch into a game of tonsil tennis, why not leave the tongue out of it at first? When you think about making out, the tongue immediately comes to mind, but kissing can be just as sensual and erotic if it's done with a closed mouth. If you go down that road you can introduce tongue slowly. Hopefully your partner will follow suit, and the two of you can work out how to kiss together.

GROPING, TOUCHING, RUBBING

You'll probably find that as you start to get comfortable with the notion of making out, your hands will want to wander. If you're into the person who's sucking your face, chances are you'll want to go exploring — both of you will. You'll be groping over clothes to start with, feeling at boobs and legs and butts (your partner's, not your own — unless you really like your own butt).

Even while still clothed, you'll find changes happening in your bodies. Guys will often get boners and girls will get wet, and before you know it you'll be rubbing genitals together through your clothes. This has a bunch of different names, from the fairly obvious "dry humping" to the more obscure "frottage." As the two of you continue to get into the groove of each other's bodies, you'll find by nature you start to reach under clothes. If your partner is going too fast for you, say something — as in, slow down. Groping is good fun and might be all you do for a while.

FINGERING

It's all good and well putting hands in pants, but what happens when you get there? One option is fingering — stimulating your girlfriend's genitals with your fingers.

TAKE CARE OF YOUR MOUTH

There isn't enough gum or breath spray in the world to make up for not brushing and flossing daily. Flossing is especially important because all sorts of junk just sits in between your teeth and it really gets stinky. If someone is sucking face with you, you're sharing all of that nastiness with him or her. You've heard all about dental hygiene preventing gum disease. Poor dental care prevents getting action. Chew on that.

DEATH BY SMOOCHING

Just kidding — kissing doesn't usually lead to death. Well, not unless you are such an amazing kisser that the person you are kissing explodes. But just like with every element of sex, in which fluids are mixing and body parts are touching, there's the possibility of transmitting viruses or infections. Flu and the common cold are the most obvious culprits here, but you can also get those when your best friend or some dude on the train coughs on you. Two things are particular to kissing:

- **Cold sores (aka oral herpes)**: These look like pimples that have been picked at a lot and occur on the mouth. Oral herpes is a virus, and it's so contagious that most people have been infected with it by the time they become adults. There are different strains of the virus, and some cause no symptoms at all. When people are infected with the strain of herpes that causes sores, they can have flare-ups of those sores throughout their lives. (Oral herpes can be spread to the genitals, as well — so no kissing on any body part when you have a breakout!)

- **Mononucleosis (aka mono or "the kissing disease")**: Mono is passed on through saliva (so you can get it through kissing, but you can also get it through sharing a glass or food utensil with someone who has it) and occurs most often in people ages 15 to17. If you get mono, you'll have a really sore throat with infected tonsils, swollen glands in your neck, and total exhaustion. Of course, just because you have all of those symptoms doesn't mean you have mono. Only a doctor can diagnose you, usually by running blood tests.

Don't let this scare you away from kissing. But if you know someone is sick, or if you are considering hooking up with someone with a giant cold sore, save that kiss for another day.

First things first: Before even thinking about putting your fingers inside someone, it's important that you have washed your hands and that your nails are clipped and filed so there are no jagged edges. Ever had a paper cut? Imagine that, but below trouser level. Not good. Cut your nails in advance so you don't have to stop to grab a nail clipper at an inopportune moment (total mood killer).

As soon as you get your hand down there, you may notice that your girlfriend is wet. Don't feel it and go "Ewww!" and wipe your hand on the curtains. The lubrication is there for a reason. Without it you wouldn't be able to put your fingers inside, let alone anything else.

At the top of her vagina (above the urethra and the vaginal opening — see page 10 for a diagram) you'll feel the clitoral hood. The clitoris lives underneath. It likes to be rubbed gently. Every girl is different, and some respond to an up-and-down motion, others left-to-right, and some like a circular motion, others in only one direction. Experiment and see what your partner likes the best.

Then, there are the labia or "lips." Once again, different people have different reactions. Some girls are more sensitive than others, and rubbing your fingers between her labia may drive her wild, or make her just go "Meh." At the bottom of the labia is the entrance to the vagina itself. If your girlfriend is ready for it and wants you to, insert your finger here. It's best to start with one finger. With your palm facing up, raise your middle finger and gently rub against the opening. If it feels like she's ready for you to penetrate her — and you can always ask if you're not sure — start inserting your finger slowly, then gently pulling in and out. Don't thrust it deep inside her. Deeper doesn't mean better, and it can be uncomfortable. If the opening is wider, she may enjoy two fingers, but don't go adding fingers before she's ready — that's no fun for anyone. If you're really not sure what to do while you're down there, ask her what feels good. Chances are she's put her fingers in there already, and even if she hasn't, she'll let you know what feels right.

HAND JOBS

This is when you stimulate your boyfriend's penis with your hand. When you first touch a penis, it'll feel like a hard rod of flesh, but just because it seems solid doesn't mean you should treat it like an iron bar. It's sensitive just like a vagina (though not as sensitive as a vagina), and holding it too tightly or rubbing it vigorously can cause pain and friction burns. If the guy has a foreskin, it will move back and forth allowing you to give him a hand job without worrying about the friction. If the guy doesn't have a foreskin, you'll find that his penis may need lubrication to allow the motion. Some people choose to spit on or lick their hand before attempting to give a hand job, others use lubes that are light and water-based, like K-Y. Lotion works as long as it is mild, unscented, and kept away from the tip of the penis, (you don't want to get it into the urethra). You could also use a guy's pre-cum as lubrication.

While it seems that the options for performing a hand job are restricted to up and down, it doesn't have to be as simple as that. For one thing, the most sensitive part of the penis is the head, so you should give that part some extra attention. Try alternating between a harder and softer grip, using different hands (or both), or gently playing with his balls with one hand while stroking the penis with the other. There is a whole world of possibilities! Penises are much easier to understand than vaginas, so you'll probably figure out how to pleasure your guy in no time. (But if you don't, he probably won't mind if you keep practicing.)

WHAT IS PRE-CUM?

When a guy gets aroused, he sometimes releases a bit of pre-ejaculatory fluid (i.e., pre-cum) sometime between arousal and ejaculation. Pre-cum is produced to help keep the urethra healthy and lubricated, and it helps the sperm make its way out of the body. Some guys release a lot and others very little, and both are normal. Pre-cum may carry in it sperm that was left in the urethra from past sex or masturbation, so one can, in fact, get pregnant from it.

HOW SAFE IS IT?

While fingering and hand jobs are certainly lower risk than oral or penetrative sex in regards to sexually transmitted infections (see Chapter 7 for more on these), you can still catch a skin-to-skin STI from any of these things. So, always be careful while making any kind of sexual skin-to-skin contact, wash your hands both before and after they come into contact with a penis or a vagina, and don't engage in any acts of foreplay if you know that one of you is infected with anything.

ANAL PLAY

You've learned all about how to use the front bits, but what about the stuff around back? You may be surprised to learn that a butt can play a part in more than just anal sex. If you and your partner are fooling around you may want to involve the booty in your foreplay.

Anal play can simply be touching the anus, or it can involve inserting fingers into it. This can be done with a single finger, two fingers, or a sex toy. Boys have a gland in their butt called the prostate, which when stimulated correctly can cause the guy to orgasm. It's not something that you should suggest on a first date, but it's worth knowing if you want to experiment. Girls don't have a prostate, but sometimes girls like being butt-fingered too. Once again, it's a person-by-person preference, and you never really know what you like 'til you try it. Unfortunately, your butt doesn't lubricate itself. (If it does, you have some kind of medical issue, so see a doctor.) So if you or your partner likes this, use a little bit of lubrication. And never move the hand from the butt to the genitals without washing first or you risk infection.

STIMULATING EROGENOUS POINTS

You don't have to limit your foreplaying to what's in your pants. Both male and female bodies have erogenous zones, which are areas that like to be touched. There are obvious ones. Nipples are sensitive for both boys and girls. Necks are another, and they like to be breathed on and kissed. Some people will be aroused by their feet being rubbed, others like the small of their back to be touched, some like nibbling on their earlobe, and others like having the ear hole itself licked. And some people have erogenous zones in other places, too (part of the fun of getting to know someone is finding out where they liked to be touched). Just don't make any assumptions. If your last girlfriend liked you slobbering on her ear, the next one may find that gross. And nothing ruins a mood more than having to wipe a load of spit out of your ear if that's not your thing. So go slow when hunting down erogenous zones, and pay close attention to your partner's response.

GETTING CUDDLY

Cuddling and touching affectionately are great ways to show that special someone that you want to be close and that you enjoy the way his or her body feels. This is not only great foreplay, but also a great way to be intimate after sex or fooling around. Touching, whether it's hugging, massaging, or even lightly drawing with your fingers on a person's skin, is very sensual.

NOBODY HAS EVER DIED OF BLUE BALLS!

If you are a guy, you know that it can be a bit painful when you are anticipating an orgasm and the sexy stuff stops happening. Technically, it is called vasocongestion, but if you're experiencing this sensation, you are probably not interested in the technical terminology.

What is happening is that all that blood that flowed to your penis and testicles to create your erection (see page 12) has been there for a while and your body has been stimulated into thinking there would be an orgasm. When you stop before the orgasm, the blood still sits there making your balls feel heavy. The pain can range from mild to the equivalent of getting kicked in the stomach.

If you're wondering where the term blue balls comes from, it's because the blood that's been in the scrotum for a while loses oxygen and can sometimes give the appearance of a bluish tint. Sure, it is really uncomfortable to have to stop messing around when your penis feels like it needs to explode, but if your partner wants to stop, you need to listen.

If it's really bad, you can massage your testicles, which may decrease the severity of the sensation, or find a bathroom and finish the deed yourself. Or you can live witha bit of discomfort and wait for it to go away.

By the way, girls can have this same feeling. Their genitals also fill with blood when they are turned on, and if they stay turned on with no release it can cause things to feel heavy and achy. Society has yet to invent a term for that. Blue clit just never caught on.

CREATING A MOOD

Ambiance is extremely important. If you're going to be intimate with your boyfriend or girlfriend, you need a nice, romantic atmosphere in which you and your partner can relax and feel comfortable and sexy. This doesn't mean putting candles on the dashboard of your car before you start making out. Here are some tips for creating a mood:

- Make a CD/mp3 playlist of romantic songs that you think your partner would like.

- Dim the lights and set some candles out in your room (but don't leave them under the drawn curtains).

- Cook dinner for your partner. If you aren't a culinary genius, make something simple, like pasta. If you want to be adventurous, practice making your bf/gf's favorite recipe ahead of time. You can even put together a simple picnic. •

Q & A

Q. I am a 16-year-old guy and make-out sessions with my girlfriend are starting to get more and more intense. I think she is ready to go to third base, but what if she wants to go for more once that happens? What should I do?

A. Third base is a spot where just about anything could happen: You could move on to score, you could get sent back to the field if the batter strikes out, or you could pass out from dehydration and need electrolytes. (OK, that last part isn't likely to happen when you are fooling around, but baseball is a summer sport after all. It gets hot out there.)

The thing about third base is that it's a dangerous spot to be in, because that's when people start getting really stupid about safety. When you're at third, you're all heated up and not thinking straight. So, if you haven't already established with your partner how you feel about having intercourse (whether or not you're ready yet), or if you haven't discussed the risks and how to protect yourselves, this is not the time to do it. Stay at third base for now and wait to have sex until a time when you're better prepared and have thought the decision through.

Q. When my boyfriend and I start to kiss, I can tell that he has a boner, but he doesn't do anything more than kiss me. He says that his mom says that he has to be respectful of me, and I think he is not being respectful because I really want to take things further and he doesn't seem to get it. How can I get him to move past kissing me without having to make every single move?

A. The best way to handle problems like this is to talk about them at a completely different time than when they are going on. Making out can put the pressure on, and if your boy is already visibly excited, it isn't the best time to lay into him about how he needs to step up the groping. It sounds like he is really nervous to take things too far, and rightly so. Boys are a lot like the Incredible Hulk when it comes to sexual excitement. No, they don't throw cars or change color, but they can become easily overcome with physical desire, and it can be hard for them to not want to go from zero to 60 really fast.

Luckily, plenty of moms out there remember their own days of necking with boys, and they train their sons to be mindful of how far is too far. The next time the two of you are hanging out, fully clothed and boner-free, have a discussion with your boyfriend about the sort of things you like. You don't have to say that he is doing anything wrong. Instead you can talk about how you'd like to be touched and what your boundaries and limits are. If you help establish all the yes's and no's, he'll have less to worry about.

Also, stop disrespecting him: You may be ready to go further, but because of nerves or even personal beliefs he may need a little bit more time. If he tells you he is not there yet, give him some breathing room and stay on first base.

Q. I went out with this girl and we went pretty far, but then she wanted to stop and I did. The next day at school she told everyone everything that we had done together, but she said that I couldn't get hard and that was why we stopped. I don't want to be rude and blab my mouth off about what really happened, but it isn't fair that she is making things up or even that she is talking about stuff we did at all. What can I do?

A. First of all, we commend you for sticking to your morals and stopping when she asked you to stop. You are right when you say it is wrong for this girl to talk about the things the two of you did (or didn't do) together. You are also right to not try to get back at her by giving all the down-and-dirty details yourself.

So, why is she doing this? She could be mean-spirited and shallow, but it is more likely that she feels weird about what happened and wants to make sure you don't complain to people that she wouldn't "put out." You probably don't feel much like talking to her right now, but really the best way to handle this situation is to confront her privately. If you can find some way to pull her aside and tell her that what she is saying isn't cool, you should do that. If she is berating you in front of other people, it is more than fine for you to calmly tell her in front of these people that she's not being truthful and that that isn't cool, though you might also just ignore the comments, as people might believe her if they see you getting defensive.

Whatever you do, don't change the fact that when a girl asks you to stop, you stop. Eventually, you'll meet a more mature girl who appreciates a guy who's a gentleman.

Q. Why does kissing feel so good and get me so worked up?

A. *It sounds like you've found yourself a good kisser! For any of us who have ever had a bad kiss, we appreciate the value of the kind of kiss that feels great. Kissing can be one of the best parts of sexuality. It is a way to comfort, greet, or part with someone — or to show them you really want to get down. When you kiss someone, it is like your mouth is figuring out what the rest of the person's body will do when it connects with yours. Kissing is natural and biological, and it is no wonder we like it so much.*

When we kiss we are tasting another person, and getting a whopping dose of their pheromones, which is the fragrance our bodies make that can impact our sexual attractiveness to another person. Also, because the skin on your lips is much thinner than on other parts of your body, your lips are very sensitive. Your lips fill with blood when you are aroused, making them feel warm and tingly when you kiss.

THERE ARE NO STUPID QUESTIONS —
EXCEPT FOR THIS ONE

Q. If I want to make it to third base on the first date, does it help to bring a baseball bat?

CHAPTER 6

ORAL, VAGINAL, AND ANAL SEX

You're Going to Put That Where?

The first type of sex most of us learn about in health class (or on late-night cable TV) is the traditional making-babies type of sex: a penis in a vagina. Of course, there are an awful lot of ways to have sex. But since no one is sure if armpit sex is for real or just an urban legend, we'll concentrate on the top three: oral, anal, and vaginal. Each of these types of sex comes with its own pleasures and pitfalls. If you are sexually active, it's important to know what you're doing so you can be safe wherever your penis, vagina, mouth, or hand end up.

VAGINAL SEX

This is the most common of all the types of sex. This is the way men and women have been doing it since the dawn of time. It's also the way babies are made. (If you don't know how babies are made by vaginal sex, please go immediately to page 13 for a crash course on reproduction.) Lesbians also have vaginal sex, though it plays out a little bit differently. We'll get to that later.

STRAIGHT VAGINAL SEX

The recipe for man-woman vaginal sex is as follows: a penis, a vagina, a condom, a pelican. "Why a pelican?" you ask. Well, you'll need something to store your condoms in, and pelicans have large beaks. A drawer, pocket, or purse will also do.

You may also want to use a lubricant to help ease the penis into the vagina. Not everyone needs lube, but it can be useful to have some just in case. Always use a water-based lubricant (like K-Y or Astroglide) because oil-based lubes (like Vaseline, mineral oil, and hand lotion) break down the material condoms are made of. Water-based lubes are also better for the health of the vagina.

Before attempting sex, you should get both of your bodies ready by engaging in foreplay, which you should have read about in Chapter 5 (unless you just skipped that part and flipped right to this chapter — cheater). Foreplay helps make sure that the penis is sufficiently hard and that the vagina is sufficiently lubricated, which will help make sex more comfortable for both of you. (It also makes sex safer because lubrication helps prevent a condom from breaking due to friction, and also prevents small tears from occurring in the walls of the vagina, which would make the girl more susceptible to contracting a disease.)

When you are ready to have sex, put the condom on the penis (see pages 107-108 in Chapter 7 for how best to do this!).

Here are the primary things to think about with straight vaginal sex.

1. POSITIONS

Most first timers start with the girl on her back with her legs apart and the guy laying on top of her. This is called missionary position. While it would be lovely for our genitals to know their way around our partner's body, you may find it a little hard to get the penis in the right place, so feel free to use a hand to guide it.

Although the missionary position is common, that doesn't mean it is the best position for you. Since all of our bodies are very different inside and out, not all people fit together exactly the same way. If one position isn't working for you and you are still in the mood to keep going, there are many other positions to try. Apart from being safe, the most important thing to remember when you start having sex is that it should feel comfortable to both people. Sex that hurts isn't fun for anyone.

2. SPEED

Guys: It's important to remember that you're putting a penis in a place that may not have met one before, so be gentle. Don't shove it in hard and fast — slow and steady wins the sex race. And move at a speed that both of you enjoy. Chances are if it's your first time with a person you'll want to take your time to adapt to the new body attached to you. Then you can vary your speed throughout. It cannot be stressed enough that you should pay attention to the person you are having sex with. From time to time ask your partner if everything feels OK and whether you should try anything different.

IT HAS TO BE CONSENSUAL

Sex or foreplay should be consensual every time you have it, no matter what kind of sex it is and who you are having it with. Consensual means both people agree to have it, while they are sober, with no doubt or questions. If it is not consensual, it is considered sexual abuse or rape. Approximately one out of every five girls and one out of every 10 boys is sexually abused before they reach adulthood, so it is a pretty big issue. And for teens, you also need to think about date rape, which is when a person is forced to have sex by someone they know (often someone they are on a date with or met at a party). If someone forces you to have sex against your will — even if you say no at the last minute, have had sex with them before, or have already started to have sex — it is considered rape and is not your fault.

While it is never your fault if someone abuses you, there are precautions you can take to narrow the chances. Instead of going out alone with someone you don't know well, go on group dates. And don't get wasted at parties or on dates so that your head is always clear. You can also take self-defense classes, which can help to ward off unwanted advances. And if you have been sexually abused in any way, talk to a trusted adult or counselor about it, or see the resources in the back of the book for numbers to call.

LESBIAN VAGINAL SEX

Now that we've talked all about penis-vagina sex, let's discuss girl-on-girl sex. Two girls can have vaginal sex in a few different ways. With each of those ways safety is still very important.

1. PENETRATION OR STIMULATION WITH A TOY

One way girls have vaginal sex with each other is by using toys like dildos (a fake rubber or silicone penis), vibrators, or even strap-on harnesses. With dildos, one person inserts the dildo into the other's vagina. If you are having this type of vaginal sex, see the tips on page 85 regarding speed and positions. Insert toys gently and make sure your partner is comfortable with the rhythm and depth. Vibrators are often used as stimulation without penetration, and they're used at different pressures in different areas.

Always make sure the toys are absolutely clean before insertion, even if the toy is used by only one person, because it can still lead to various kinds of infections. Most toys come with instructions about how to wash them so read them carefully. Lots of people opt to cover the toy with a new condom each time they use it because that is a good way to make sure it's always clean.

2. MANUAL SEX
Another type of vaginal sex for girls is manual sex, which consists of practices such as fingering (see pages 71 and 73) and fisting (see page 88). These practices are often considered foreplay for straight couples, but for lesbians, they are also considered to be full-on sex.

3. SCISSORING
If girls are scissoring, they are laying with their legs interlocked and their vaginas rubbing together. Many lesbian couples describe

DO GIRLS HAVE MORE SKILLS?
A lot of people assume that if two girls are having sex, they'll intuitively know how to please each other because they have the same parts. This, along with the thinking that all women are born knowing how to bake pies and burp babies, is a myth. All girls are different in terms of what they like, and even in lesbian relationships it can take a little trial and error to see what works best.

WHAT IS FISTING?

Fisting is kind of what it sounds like — and kind of not. It does involve putting a whole hand in a vagina (or anus), but the fingers are typically straight, with fingertips touching — not curled up in a fist shape. The person doing the fisting will (using lubrication and a rubber glove for safety) start with one finger, and then, with the other person's permission, gradually add another, and another. Fisting is not for everyone. A whole hand inside someone can actually be wider than a penis, and it can be uncomfortable for some people. Fisting is considered an advanced-level sex act (and therefore not necessarily something to try right off the bat) that carries a significant amount of risk, including the possibility of excess bleeding (due to a muscle tear) and a higher risk of contracting an STI. It is something that has to be approached with extreme gentleness, and the partners must have total trust in each other as well as excellent communication, so both know exactly what feels good and when to stop.

this as the most intimate thing they can do in bed together. There is currently no way to practice safe sex while scissoring because the genitals are touching. That's risky — so scissoring should happen only in a long-term, committed relationship after both partners have been tested for STIs.

ANAL SEX

This involves putting a penis (or something like a penis) into a butt. This is often thought to be a type of sex reserved for gay men, but straight couples also do it, and lesbian couples may do it using a toy.

Anal sex is more complicated than vaginal and oral sex, and you have to be really, really sure you are up for it. It takes a lot of preparation and can also cause pain. Even if you are a gay male, there is no rule that you should be having anal sex. So consider this: If you are offering anal sex only because you are being pressured into it, or because you think it is a more "virginal" act than other kinds of sex, don't do it. It's never good to do anything because you are being pressured, and it is still sex — there's nothing virginal about it.

Also, if you are the person who really wants to have anal sex and your partner is 100 percent opposed to it, you have no choice but to be very respectful and let the issue rest. Maybe one day he or she will feel comfortable enough to try it and will let you know. Until that happens, don't try to manipulate your partner into doing anything he or she doesn't want to do.

PREPARATION
If you both consent to try it, anal sex requires more preparation than other types of sex. You'll need:

1. DURABLE CONDOMS
You need good, strong condoms. Make sure to check the expiration dates and if the packaging is torn, don't use the condom. Not ones from the bargain bin. Regular latex condoms that fit properly will do the trick. If you are sensitive to latex, you can use polyurethane condoms; in the past, some have reported that wearing polyurethane condoms makes you feel like you've just stuck a plastic sack on your wiener, but this type of condom has gotten better over the years.

2. LUBRICATION.
Unlike the mouth or vagina, your butt doesn't lubricate itself. In addition to the condom, which will possibly be lubricated, a water-based lube will make the whole process much easier. Remember: Lubricant needs to be water-based because oil-based lubes break down the material condoms are made of.

You may be tempted to buy certain lubricants that claim to numb the anus and make anal sex pain-free. It is not recommended that you use these products be-

cause you need to be aware of any pain you are feeling. Pain is your body's way of telling you that something is wrong.

3. A COMFORTABLE AND RELAXING LOCATION THAT HAS A BATHROOM.

Definitely don't have butt sex in your mom's car or any location which does not have a place nearby where you can clean up afterward.

GO IN STAGES

Put a dollop of lubricant on a finger and (gently!) slide a finger into the other person's butt. Slow and not too deep to start with; the butt can be a pretty sensitive place and the muscles can tense up pretty tight. After the person feels relaxed enough with one finger, try two, and if that goes well, put a third finger under the other two. Three fingers is about the width of the average penis, so if you can slide your fingers back and forth easily enough, chances are your partner is ready for the real thing.

POSITIONS

While it is possible to have anal in the missionary position (lying down, facing each other), it's easier to start anal sex with the person about to be penetrated lying on their front or on all fours with their back arched, and butt in the air.

WHY DO IT?

With all of this talk about preparation and pain, you may be wondering why people even bother with anal sex. Guys have something inside of their butts called a prostate gland, which, when stimulated with a finger, toy, or penis, feels good and can even lead to orgasm. Some women also have erogenous areas in their butts. And the giver may like it because of the way the anus feels around the penis. Anal sex is also a common way of making love in the gay community, and can be as romantic as any other type of sex. And some people like it for other reasons altogether. Our bodies have different hot spots, and for some that hot spot is in the butt.

WHAT ABOUT POOP?

Anal sex is all about something going in where something usually comes out. That being said, you may be wondering how big a part feces plays in the whole process. There are two important things to keep in mind when it comes to back-dooring it.

1. Never put a penis (same goes for hands and sex toys) into a vagina or mouth after it has been in a butt. Poop is full of bacteria — that's why we don't eat it — and if that bacteria gets into a mouth or a vagina, you are asking for trouble. The person on the receiving end could get very ill, contracting anything from parasites to a urinary tract infection (no fun!). If you decide to move from one spot to the other, make sure to change your condom and wash your hands/penis/sex toy.

2. Go to the bathroom first, or at least be sure that there is no feces on deck wanting to come out. The presence of feces in the lower colon, which is the part of the butt the penis would be poking in and out of, can make the whole ordeal pretty darn uncomfortable. Some people have compared the feeling of anal sex to "pooping in reverse" so the last thing you need is to have more junk in your trunk.

TIPS...

...FOR THE RECEIVER

Try some different positions to find the one that feels most comfortable for you. Some people lay on their bellies, sides, get on their knees, or even lay on their backs. Don't forget to breathe, relax as much as you can, and always tell your partner if things don't feel right. Sometimes anal sex can lead to small tears or bleeding in your butt. If it happens every time you partake in anal, it may be worth going to a doctor, as it is possible to get an infection.

...FOR THE GIVER

Even if you want to go fast, ease into it and maintain a speed that is comfortable for the boy or girl who has been kind enough to let you in through the back door. Listen to your partner's noises, or if anything is said, and if you notice that your condom has any issues at all, stop what you are doing immediately.

ORAL SEX

This is the sex that has been giving guys and girls sore jaws for a bajillion years at least.

Oral sex is using your mouth on someone's genitals, and if both people are comfortable it can be as enjoyable as (if not more than) other kinds of sex. The three basic kinds of oral sex are cunnilingus (aka, going down on someone, muff-diving, eating someone out, or tipping the velvet); fellatio (aka, blow job, giving head, or sucking off); and anilingus (aka, rimming, eating butt, or tossing salad). A 69 is when the two partners lie face-to-groin and give each other oral at the same time.

People like oral sex because it is a very intimate way of sharing your body with someone, and also because most people think it feels really good. Because no penetration is involved, it's also a gentler form of sex. But just because there's no penis going in a vagina or butt, doesn't mean you shouldn't protect yourself. You can still transfer STIs (like cold sores — Virus I) through oral sex.

When giving oral sex to a girl, you could use a dental dam to prevent the transfer of an STI. These are thin, flat sheets of polyurethane or latex that are laid flat against the whole vulva — which includes both the vaginal opening and the clitoris — during sex. These can be held in place and they often come flavored, too, so you can satisfy your sweet tooth while satisfying your girlfriend. If you don't have a dental dam, you can carefully cut a condom lengthwise and use that instead.

When giving oral sex to a guy, you can use condoms to prevent the penis from catching anything from your mouth, or vice versa. You can use condoms that are flavored or plain, but don't lick a spermicidal condom.

GIVING ORAL SEX TO A GIRL

The phrase eating out is not a description of how to perform oral sex. That will end badly, in screaming. The vagina is sensitive and requires a little bit of delicacy. In fact, between a girl's waist and her thighs there are many areas that may like to be kissed, and it's good to start there. Before you dive in, take a look at what you've got in front of you. Locate her labia, which are more often referred to as the lips, and the clitoris, which exists underneath the clitoral hood (see the diagram on page 10). Let your tongue explore the various areas and see what she likes and dislikes. Remember not to get carried away with speed and force. Start off slow and sensual, reacting to her body. It may not be particularly comfortable, but occasionally look up to see if she is enjoying herself. And if you're not sure if she's enjoying it, just ask. But don't talk with your mouth full.

GIVING ORAL SEX TO A DUDE

Perhaps you've been told you need to fit the entire penis into your mouth and then bob away like you're agreeing to something emphatically. If that's what you've heard, you've been misinformed. The most sensitive part of the penis is the head. That doesn't mean you should ignore everything else. You can use your hand to help you guide the speed and depth, and you can even try touching all of the other merchandise below the belt to see how your boy reacts. Everything around the penis can feel good if touched just the right way, so be gentle and give it a go.

But remember: Penises don't like teeth. A little nibbling along the shaft of the penis may get a guy excited, but the head of the penis is very sensitive and knocking teeth against it can make a guy weep in agony. You can avoid too much scraping by using your lips to cover your teeth.

GIVING ORAL SEX TO A BUTT

When giving or receiving anilingus, refer to the same cleanliness rules of all sex. Do make sure that the butt is clean and make sure to clean your mouth before kissing or licking any other part of the person's body. In addition to that, use a dental dam, the same thing you'd use for vaginal oral sex (see pages 92-93). If you're reading this and you are confused about why anyone would want to lick a butt, it may not be for you. Some people really find it an enjoyable sensation and a way to express to the other person that they like all parts of them.

PLEASING YOUR PARTNER

While it does seem that some people know exactly what to do, most of us are not born sexual dynamos. This is good news. It means that even if your boyfriend/girlfriend isn't immediately gifted in the bedroom, he or she is capable of learning — and so are you!

OH, CUM ON!

People put a lot of importance on the orgasm during sex. But as discussed earlier, it's not the most important part of sex. If you have one, great. If you don't, focus on enjoying the actual sex. The orgasm may come next time — but it won't if you keep stressing over it.

And not everybody reaches orgasm the same way. For some, orgasm is reached most easily through oral sex; for others penetrative sex or mutual masterbation. That goes for both guys and girls. Some people need to be

THE MYSTERIOUS G-SPOT

There is a region called the G-spot that is thought to be more sensitive than other parts of the vagina. It is said to be an area inside the vagina on the upper wall about two to three inches in. It is easiest to stimulate this with your fingers, and if you happen to have them inside your girl-friend already you can try to see how she feels if you stimulate this area. Some women say that this is the spot for sexual satisfaction; others say it doesn't do much for them. Some activists and doctors worry that putting emphasis on the existence of the G-spot is a bad idea, because it puts a lot of pressure on women who might not have any sexual response related to having anything done to this part of their body. They worry that it puts pressure on people who want to please women because they're always trying to find the G-spot. There's been a lot of research, and it all seems to indicate that every single person is completely different. If you have a G-spot, great. If you don't, no big deal. Like anything with sex, it really depends on the person.

How about a little bit of history? The G-spot is named after Dr. Grafenberg, a German Jewish doctor and scientist who not only invented the IUD and had a pleasure-inducing part of women's bodies named after him, he also escaped Nazi death camp imprisonment because a woman named Margaret Sanger paid a large ransom to save him and bring him to America. And who is Margaret Sanger? She's the woman who popularized the term "birth control" and started the organization that has now become Planned Parenthood.

in a certain position to orgasm, or to masturbate. Some girls need their clitorises rubbed. Some people like to have their nipples touched in just the right way. It's a really personal thing. Work out what works best for both of you. Also remember that two people rarely orgasm at the exact same time, so don't trip if your partner doesn't have an orgasm when you do or vice versa. •

Q. This guy I'm seeing likes my boobs, and I mean really likes them. He keeps trying to put his thing between them, like he's having sex. It seems weird. What should I do?

A. *As we all know, some guys are quite fond of boobs and rightly so — boobs are great. It's perfectly normal for a guy you're intimate with to want to rub himself against you, whether hand or feet, legs or boobs. As long as you enjoy him humping you (and he cleans up after himself), it's a totally normal thing to do. It is also a lot safer than the types of sex mentioned in this chapter and definitely won't get you preggers! If it actually makes you uncomfortable, let him know that you want him to stop. As with all sexual activity, it's important that both partners enjoy everything they take part in, and this is no different.*

Q. My boyfriend and I have tried to have sex a few times, but it hurts. What's wrong? Is it possible that his penis is too big for my vagina? Or could it be something else?

A. It is possible that your boyfriend's penis is too large for your vagina. With variances in both penis size and vaginal depth, some bodies just don't fit together. While you can try different positions and ask him to be very gentle, you may not be able to get his penis all the way inside of you, though using a dildo on your own may help you get more used to the size and to the basic sensation of having something in there.

Other factors that may come into play are that you are tense for some reason (worried about privacy or pregnancy, for instance) and cannot produce enough natural lubrication; he may be entering you too quickly or too soon; or, because of your nervousness, your vaginal muscles tense up too much for penetration. Any of these things can cause sex to be painful.

Pain could also be an indication that something is not quite right physically. You could have a vaginal infection, which may or may not be a sexually transmitted infection (see pages 112–114). You could also have a condition that some girls have called vaginismus, which causes your vaginal muscles to involuntarily spasm, making sex very uncomfortable or impossible. Vaginal pain would then also be common during attempted pelvic exams. There are also certain nerve conditions that cause pain in the vulvar area that could make sex painful. These conditions are usually only temporary, but they do need treatment. If you suspect something is wrong "down there," see a doctor as soon as you can.

Q. When giving oral sex to a guy, how do you know if you should spit or swallow?

A. First, we'll assume that you are in a monogamous relationship and have been tested for STIs, and that's why you're not using condoms for oral sex. You're also making sure that you don't have a cold sore when you give oral sex because that could become genital herpes for your boyfriend. So, if all of that is clear, then we can move on to the answer.

Spitting or swallowing cum during oral sex is largely a matter of personal taste. (Yeah... taste.) When you swallow, it gives you a chance to leave the penis in your mouth longer, possibly prolonging the blow job at a time when the penis is feeling really happy. It also may be a way of telling your boyfriend that you like his penis so much that you would gladly swallow his cum. These are reasons that people are sometimes big supporters of swallowing.

However, not everyone likes to swallow and not every guy even enjoys coming in a mouth. If you are not a swallowing kind of person, there are other ways to handle the possible moment of orgasm. You can leave the room and spit in a bathroom, then rinse your mouth out. Or you can pull your mouth away as your boyfriend is about to finish and, if he likes, either let him masturbate or give him a hand job until he's done.

You don't need to have a pre-blow plan, but if you're the one giving the blow job, let your guy know where (in or out) you'd like him to finish. It is OK to stop what you're doing long enough to say a few words. If you're the one with your penis in a mouth, let the person know when you're close to coming and you can follow their lead.

THERE ARE NO STUPID QUESTIONS — EXCEPT FOR THIS ONE

Q. If I swallow a lot of sperm, will I build up my body's tolerance for it so I won't get pregnant during sex?

CHAPTER 7

PROTECTING YOURSELF

How to Steer Clear of Disease

If you are a teen and having sex of any kind, you need to protect yourself. That doesn't mean you should trot around with a bodyguard. It means you need to make sure you don't get or give an STI or STD to anyone. (It also means preventing pregnancy — but we'll cover that more in the next chapter.)

STIs and STDs are not some new text message slang. An STI (sexually transmitted infection) is an infection transferred by sexual contact, and an STD (sexually transmitted disease), is what the infection is called once symptoms appear. There are two names because a person can have an infection without symptoms and still spread the infection to someone else, who can get the full-blown disease. Bottom line, of course, is that you don't want to have either. Here's some more information about what sexually transmitted infections are, how to prevent getting them, and how to deal if you already have one.

HOW STIS ARE SPREAD

STIs are spread in two ways: through skin-to-skin contact and through the exchange of bodily fluid during oral, vaginal, or anal sex. They can be spread from one person's genitals (penis or vagina) to another's, and also between mouth and genitals. STIs range from minor to severe, and from curable (you can get rid of it with medicine) to treatable (you can treat the symptoms, but you'll always have the virus in your system).

KNOW YOUR STIS

Here's a rundown of some basic STIs, what they do, how you contract them, and what the treatment is for them.

HERPES SIMPLEX VIRUS I AND II (HSV I AND II)

HOW YOU GET IT: Skin-to-skin contact during vaginal, anal, or oral sex or during sexual activities in which you rub exposed skin together.

SYMPTOMS: HSV I (aka cold sores) typically appears on the mouth and HSV II typically appears on the genitals, though both can be present in either place. If you have HSV on the mouth, you'll get cold sores from time to time during an "outbreak." If you've been exposed to genital herpes, you'll most likely notice genital itching or pain followed by painful sores about two to 20 days after being infected. You may also have painful urination, fever, and headaches. However, some people who get the virus don't have any symptoms at all, so it's important to remember that you may still be infected (and contagious) without any symptoms.

TESTS: Skin swab of infected area or blood test.

TREATMENT: There is no cure for herpes, so once you have it, you have it for life. It can be treated with an antiviral medication, which will lessen the frequency and length of an outbreak and reduce the chance of spreading it to others.

HUMAN IMMUNODEFICIENCY VIRUS/AUTO IMMUNE DEFICIENCY SYNDROME (HIV/AIDS)

HOW YOU GET IT: Exchange of bodily fluids mainly through vaginal and anal sex, and, in very rare cases, oral sex. When only the virus is present, someone is considered HIV positive; after symptoms start to present themselves, the patient is considered to have AIDS.

SYMPTOMS: Symptoms usually do not occur for seven to 10 years, which makes it very easy for someone to spread HIV without knowing it. The virus affects the immune system, destroying the defense cells that fight infectious diseases in the body. People with HIV get serious infections they normally wouldn't get. Common symptoms that start to appear are recurring infections throughout the body, as well as weight loss, chronic diarrhea, white spots in the mouth, fever, fatigue, vaginal infections, growths and open sores on the skin, and night sweats. Eventually, large-scale infections and illnesses may occur, which can lead to death.

TESTS: Blood test or mouth swab.

TREATMENT: There is no cure for HIV/AIDS, but there are antiviral medications, which can boost the immune system and prolong the life of the infected person and even allow an active lifestyle. The drugs can have severe side effects. Also, the disease can become resistant to treatment. The fact that HIV/AIDS is not curable and fatal is why prevention is so important. There are currently some experimental emergency drugs to prevent infection right after exposure, but they are not widely available yet.

HUMAN PAPILLOMAVIRUS (HPV)

HOW YOU GET IT: Skin-to-skin contact during vaginal, oral, or anal sex.

SYMPTOMS: HPV is a virus (with more than 100 strains), some of which can cause abnormal cell growth in the cervix and even, in some cases, cancer. Other strains are more likely to cause genital warts. For girls, the warts are on or near the vulva, vagina, cervix, or anus.

In guys, they are on or near the penis, scrotum, or anus. Warts can be any size, are usually whitish or flesh-colored, and are sometimes hard to see. You can also be infected with HPV and not have genital warts; in this case, it is still possible to pass the virus along to someone else.

TESTS: Swab test of the cervix for women (also known as a Pap smear). There is not a test for men.

TREATMENT: Usually the body will cure the infection in one or two years, but for those who get secondary medical problems such as warts and cancer, those things have to be treated more aggressively. There is a fairly new vaccination recommended for people between the ages of nine and 26 that is effective at preventing certain strains of the virus, so do ask your doctor about this. Previously this vaccination was only available for females, but now it is available for everyone.

GONORRHEA

HOW YOU GET IT: Exchange of bodily fluids during vaginal, anal, or oral sex.

SYMPTOMS: This is a bacterium that grows in the warm, moist reproductive tract and results in painful urination, smelly discharge, fever, and severe abdominal pain. It can also lead to sterility or the inability to reproduce. The same bacterium can grow in your mouth, throat, eyes, and anus.

TESTS: Swab test of the mouth, anus, vagina, cervix, or from the discharge of the penis.

TREATMENT: Antibiotics.

SYPHILIS

HOW YOU GET IT: Skin-to-skin contact during vaginal, anal, or oral sex or by rubbing genitals together.

SYMPTOMS: This starts with painless sores (in the spot where the contact was made with the infected person's body) 10 days to three months after sexual contact. Sometimes there are sores inside the anus or vagina that go unnoticed. Three weeks to six months after contact there can be flulike illness with rashes. If untreated, syphilis can eventually lead to blindness, brain deterioration, shooting pains in the limbs, loss of feeling in parts of the body, damage to the organs, and even death.

TESTS: Swab test on areas with visible open sores (penis, vagina, anus) or a blood test. If more advanced, spinal fluid test.

TREATMENT: Antibiotics. But if left untreated, some of the damage to the body may be irreversible.

SCABIES

HOW YOU GET IT: Skin-to-skin contact during sexual activity, as well as from infected clothing or bedding. (Scabies is spread by more than just sexual contact, so if someone has it this doesn't mean they got it from sex necessarily.)

SYMPTOMS: Scabies occurs when very small insects called mites burrow into the skin, laying eggs and producing secretions that cause a rash of small red bumps and blisters, most likely to show up on the waist, knees, webs of fingers, genitals, and elbows first but will eventually involve the whole body.

TESTS: Medical examination of the skin.

TREATMENT: Medicated soap and decontamination of all bedding and clothing.

CHLAMYDIA

HOW YOU GET IT: Exchange of bodily fluids during vaginal, anal, or oral sex.

SYMPTOMS: Like gonorrhea, chlamydia is caused by bacteria. It's one of the most common STIs because 75 percent of women and 50 percent of men show no symptoms (and spread it unknowingly). When symptoms are present they usually show up one to three weeks after exposure, and they include painful urination, abdominal cramping especially during sex, itching or swollen testicles, and genital discharge.

TESTS: Urine test or swab test of the mouth, anus, or cervix.

TREATMENT: Antibiotics. If untreated, chlamydia can lead to pelvic inflammatory disease (PID) or sterility/infertility.

THRICHOMONIASIS

HOW YOU GET IT: Exchange of bodily fluids during penis-to-vagina or vulva-to-vulva sex.

SYMPTOMS: Caused by a little parasite that usually lives in the vagina (in women) and in the urethra (for men). The symptoms usually show up within five to 28 days of being exposed to an infected person, and include slight burning after urination, foamy vaginal discharge, and itching and burning in the vagina.

TESTS: Swab test of the vagina or of the secretions from the penis.

TREATMENT: Prescription medications.

PUBIC LICE (CRABS)

HOW YOU GET IT: Skin-to-skin (or, really, hair-to-hair) contact during sexual activity. Just like head lice, these can also live in fabrics, making it possible to catch them from someone's infested clothing, towel, or bedding. If you are within their proximity they will jump on to you.

SYMPTOMS: Pubic lice are tiny insects that live by sucking blood from their host (you), causing itching and a presence of eggs and bugs in pubic hair. You'll start to notice symptoms usually within one to three weeks.

TESTS: Just by looking at it. Pubic lice look like small flakes of skin, and their eggs look like gray or white dots that hold onto strands of pubic hair.

TREATMENT: There are special lice-killing shampoos specifically for crabs that should take care of the bugs on your body, but you'll also need to thoroughly clean all your bedding, towels, and clothing to kill all the lice and their eggs.

HOW TO AVOID GETTING AN STI

Since some STIs can be transmitted through skin-to-skin contact, you are more likely to get an STI than to get knocked up (especially if you are a guy!). With the STI rates as high as they are and the ease with which some of them are passed along, it is a wonder people don't seal themselves off in bubbles and have sex only with robots. However, robots are nowhere near as sexy as that hottie in your algebra class, and until they can make a bubble that looks good with any outfit, we'll all be exposed to the open air.

The best protection beyond not exchanging bodily fluids with anyone is to use condoms. Be sure that you put the condom on properly and that you use them for anal, oral, and vaginal sex. Girls, get familiar with dental dams, those thin sheets of latex or polyurethane that you put over your vagina before your boyfriend or girlfriend goes down on you.

KNOW YOUR CONDOMS

Not all condoms are created equal. If you take a look at any major condom manufacturer's website you will find a whole slew of options. So how do you know which rubbers are the best for you? Consider the following.

MATERIALS

Most condoms are made of latex, a durable and safe material used for everything from theatrical makeup to rubber gloves at the hospital. Some people claim to have an allergy to latex just to avoid using a condom, but only few people are actually allergic to latex (they have itchiness, dryness, and burning when latex comes in contact with their skin). For those who are allergic, there are polyurethane condoms. Polyurethane condoms are made of a type of plastic. The plastic actually feels thinner than latex, which might end up feeling better, but it's slightly less flexible, meaning that more lubrication might be needed in order to ensure the condoms don't break. This type can also be more expensive than latex condoms. There are also sheep skin condoms, but they don't provide any protection against STIs and (ewww) are made of sheep skin. Even if you aren't a huge animal rights activist, you have to admit that skinning sheep is rude.

LUBRICATION

Condoms are available lubricated or non-lubricated, and the lubricated ones are better because they will help get the penis inside and also help prevent the condom from tearing from too much friction. If you think you'll need extra lube beyond what's on the condom, don't just reach for whatever you have lying around. Use a water-based lube because oil-based lubes will break down the condom material. Sometimes people add their own water-based lube (just a drop) inside the condom so the guy can have a little something extra.

Some condoms are also lubricated with the spermicide Nonoxynol-9, but a lot of girls are sensitive to the stuff and some studies have shown that it can lead to higher susceptibility to STIs, so you may want to re-consider using these kind of condoms.

FIT

While every man wants to buy XXL condoms, it's not recommended. If condoms don't fit properly, they don't work properly. If the fit is too loose, the condom might fall off or let all the semen ooze out. (Alternately, if the fit is too tight, the condom could tear.) Guys, if you really want girls to think you have a huge penis, you could get an XXL condom box and fill it with normal-sized condoms. Or just accept that you have a normal-sized penis. Nobody likes false advertising, and, hey, they'll find out the truth anyhow.

IT WAS A GOODYEAR!

Historians tell us that the first condoms were made of linen, fine leather, and animal intestines (sexy!). But the first mass-produced condoms were made of latex and put on the market in 1843. The company that made them was none other than Goodyear, though these days Goodyear is more famous for its tires.

EXTRAS

Condoms come in many colors and, for oral sex, in different flavors. There is even some variation in the shape of the tips. Some are ribbed, which means they have some extra bumps on the outside and supposedly feel better for girls. There are even condoms that have vibrating rings at the base. Condoms have come a long way over the years. Find a favorite condom, and don't ever go without it.

HOW DO I USE A CONDOM?

Hey, guys! Condoms are super fun! It's like you get to play dress-up with your penis, again and again. If you are baffled by the best ways to use your condom as something other than a stylish new skull cap, just follow these easy tips. Soon, you'll be on your way to earning the Boy Scout Condom Master merit badge.

1. Check the condom packaging for a date. This tells you when the condom is no longer safe to use. If the condom is expired, throw it away and get a new one.
2. Open the condom. They don't work well in the foil. And open it with your hands (not your mouth or toes). Be careful of fingernails.
3. Grab the tip of the condom between your finger and thumb, making sure you push all of the air out. Place the ring around your erect penis. (Condoms don't work on a soft penis, so wait

until you're sufficiently hard to put the condom on.)

4. Gently roll the condom down to the base of your penis, taking time to appreciate how cool it is that you have such a thing protruding from your body.

5. It might be necessary to change the condom while you're still having sex, so make sure you own more than one. If you get soft during, or if you're lasting a long time, the condom might shift or get dry, making it more likely to break.

6. After sex, remove the condom while you are still erect. Don't just lay there basking in happiness — stuff can leak out of the condom as your penis shrinks back to its usual size. Grab that tip again, squeezing it so that you trap the fluid inside. Use your other hand to hold the ring and slide it off.

6. Don't flush the condom down the toilet — it's bad for plumbing and the environment. Instead, wrap it in toilet paper and chuck it in the garbage. Never use a condom twice. Apart from that being just plain gross, condoms are only effective the first go-round.

WHAT DO I DO IF IT BREAKS OR COMES OFF?

Condoms do sometimes break or come off. It's not a frequent occurrence, but it's possible. (This is a good reason to have a backup form of birth control! See more about this in the next chapter.) If it breaks, stop having sex right away. Check the area (meaning the vagina or anus) for any bits and pieces of the broken condom. Remove the condom and throw it out.

Sometimes the condom does a much more irritating thing: It comes off inside. (This is why it is good to check the ring on the base of your penis from time to time and make sure it hasn't slipped.) If it does come off inside, do the right thing and help your partner. Have them lay down

SHOULD I USE TWO?

While it may seem like two is better than one, that's not the case with condoms. Using one condom on top of another one can actually lessen the efficacy of the whole operation. Use one properly and you shouldn't need a second one until the second round.

while you insert your fingers and feel around for it, trying to grab the ring. But be gentle; you're helping to get a condom out, not exploring a cave.

If it is really stuck up in a vagina or butt, try not to panic. The girl or guy can sit on the toilet and push really hard down through the opening it got lost in (vagina or anus). It all sounds pretty uncomfortable, but if you leave the condom inside you, things will likely get infected. If you simply cannot get the condom out, have your partner call the doctor, who will have no problem finding it.

If the condom broke or came off, you are obviously now at a higher risk of getting pregnant or an STI. You should consider emergency contraception (see page 125) if you were having vaginal sex and did not use a backup method of birth control. You also need to get tested in about a week for an STI. Ideally, you should get tested again in six months.

HOW OFTEN SHOULD I GET TESTED?

If you are sexually active, you should be getting tested every six months, even if you are using condoms (which you'd better be). Condoms are a great protection against disease, but there's always a small chance of infection with a condom. And there are parts of your genitals not protected by the condom, making transmission of an STI possible in those areas. The best places to get tested are local health clinics, doctors' offices, and, if you are in college, the on-campus health center.

Sometimes the doctor will test you for one specific STI, but more than likely he or she will test you for a bunch at once. That means getting blood tests and urine tests, and getting swabbed in the cervix or vagina, or on the skin around your genitals or butt.

UH, OH, I GOT AN STI

If you think you might have an STI, the first thing you should do is get yourself to a doctor. Don't sit around blogging about it or writing emails to online health forums. The only way to know for sure is to get tested.

While it may seem embarrassing, remember that doctors have seen pretty much everything in their line of work, and they are fully equipped to help you. If you don't have health insurance, find your local health clinic. Fill out any questionnaires completely honestly, even if you think it might get you into trouble. Truthful answers about your possible drug or alcohol use are important to medical professionals, and so are answers about how often you have sex and if you use protection. Again, the in-

formation is to help diagnose the problem and treat you — not to get you into trouble with your parents.

If you test positive for something, make sure you complete the full course of medication. Why? Even if your symptoms go away sooner, the infection may still be there and could flare up again. Also, if you don't complete the full course of meds, the bugs may become more resistant and harder to treat in the future.

WHO NEEDS TO KNOW?

If you end up with an STI, the first step after getting tested and starting your treatment is to let your recent partner(s) know of your infection. Even though it's not remotely fun to have the "I'm sorry I gave you chlamydia" or "I think you may have given me herpes" conversation, it's bet-

CRAZY LAWS OF TIMES PAST

If you think your parents are nosy for looking through your room, wait until you hear about this! The Comstock Law of 1873 made it illegal for the United States Postal Service to deliver any form of contraception or any materials deemed to be "pornographic." This meant that people's mail was being opened to look for any unsuitable items and that both the senders and recipients of such items would be prosecuted. This got completely out of hand and even extended to art galleries receiving partially nude works of art from abroad. You'd think a whacked-out law like that would get shut down pretty quickly, but it wasn't until 1983 that the Supreme Court finally overruled it.

ter than anyone unknowingly continuing to spread an infection around. The important thing is to remain calm and make the conversation about information, not blame.

If you got an STI as the result of a one-time hookup with a stranger, you should do your best to find that person. You could try returning to wherever you met the person or try to contact any friends you may have in common. Modern technology also makes it a lot easier to find people even if you know little about them.

Finally, there's no pressure to do so, but you might want to tell your parents. Chances are they, or someone they know, has been in the same situation, and they can probably empathize or help if you need a shoulder to lean on. Who knows? Maybe you and your mom will have a bonding moment as she tells you about the time she got crabs. If your parents are prone to flipping out, you may decide that you don't need to give them the full details, or that a trusted aunt or older cousin is a better bet as a confidant. If you contract an STI which is incurable, like HIV/AIDS or herpes, you also need to tell any potential new sex partners before you have sex with them. Even if you are symptom free and plan to use condoms (of course), that other person needs to know that they are putting themselves at risk.

It may not be a very comfortable conversation to have, but just give them as much information as you can about the disease and how it is prevented and treated. If they are too nervous to move forward, be ready for that and just know that you did the right thing. Your disease doesn't define you, but your integrity does.

SHAME, GUILT, AND OTHER NONSENSE

One important thing to remember: An STI does not define who you are. Although there may be an unjust stigma for having picked up an STI, it happens to one out of every two people in the US in their lifetimes. It sucks to have contracted one, sure, but it won't help to beat yourself up over it. If you get one of the more easily treatable ones, see it as an important life lesson. If you contract HIV, a support group can help you feel better about the stigma around having the virus, and also help you deal with the virus itself. And, regardless, remember to use a condom from now on.

NOT ALWAYS AN STI

Before you jump to the conclusion that you or your partner is infected, consider that there are many other relatively harmless conditions that cause STI-like symptoms. Some are: ingrown hairs, yeast infections, urinary tract infections, bacterial vaginosis, an inflamed gland, or even a zit down below. Point is, don't use the internet (or this book!) to diagnose

your ailment. If something starts oozing, stinking, or causing discomfort, go to the doctor and get it checked out.

THE AGONY OF A YEAST INFECTION

A vaginal yeast infection is an irritation of the vagina and the area around it. Most women get one at some point, and even though they affect the vagina, they are not considered STIs because they are rarely contracted through sexual activity. If you have a yeast infection, you likely have itching in and around the vagina, which is sometimes accompanied by a chunky cottage cheese-like vaginal discharge that smells like unbaked bread. You may also have some redness and pain. All women have naturally occurring yeast in this area, but this infection is what happens when that yeast overthrows your vaginal government.

There are a lot of different causes of yeast infections, from stress to poor eating habits to wearing tight clothing in warm weather, being pregnant, or taking antibiotics or oral contraceptives. And even though it is not considered an STI, some doctors think that yeast infections can be passed on to sex partners — so you may want to refrain from having sex while you have one.

Guys can get one, too, but the symptoms are most obvious in girls. It can be treated with an over-the-counter medication from the drugstore, but if you've taken the full course of medication and you still have symptoms (or if you are getting them repeatedly) get thyself to a doctor.

IT HURTS WHEN I PEE

Another fairly common type of infection is a urinary tract infection (UTI). A UTI is bacterial and happens to girls more than to boys. The infection starts in the urethra (pee hole) and then moves to the bladder and possibly even the kidneys.

A UTI is often caused by bacteria from the back end (a butt) spreading to the front end (the urethra). This can happen two basic ways. One is through sex, if the in-and-out motion of the penis somehow, inadvertently, carries butt bacteria toward the urethra. It can also happen through improper wiping, if a girl wipes from back to front instead of front to back when she pees.

The symptoms of a UTI range from a burning sensation when you pee to pain in the bladder or kidney area. Another tell-tale sign is the feeling that you have to pee all the time even when you didn't drink an ultra-mega-cola. You can try to prevent a UTI by peeing after sex (this helps clean out the urethra) and always wiping front to back, as well as washing your hands before you touch your vagina. Also, remember to never allow a finger or penis to go from your butt to your vagina without being thoroughly washed. But even if you are very careful, you may still get a UTI. If you think you have one, see a health care practitioner ASAP because these get worse fast. Cranberry juice and certain herbs can be helpful, but UTIs are typically treated with antibiotics. •

Q & A

Q. I'm a gay guy and I've had sex with only two other guys. My boyfriend and I want to start having sex, but he says he won't until we both get tested for STIs. I don't think that's fair because I've been safe, but he's really hot, so I'll do it. What can I expect?

A. Good for you for having a boyfriend who's so responsible! If you guys ever split up, we know plenty of guys who'll want his number. And his test results.

You'll want to get the whole run of tests. Get your blood drawn, your butts and throats swabbed, and your urine tested. You could make it a more enjoyable experience by turning testing day into a date. The two of you can make a testing playlist, go to the clinic together, get all poked and swabby with it, and then go out for a nice dinner. This is modern romance.

Q. My girlfriend puts my condom on with her mouth, which is really sexy, but it worries me because I don't know if she is doing it right. Is there a different way to put condoms on that would make the experience sexier for both of us?

A. *Whoa. Putting the condom on with the mouth is completely off-limits. Cool trick, maybe, but stupid in terms of being safe. Condoms are fragile, and it is easy to break the condom that way. She can put it on with her hand and that can be just as fun for both of you.*

Q. I am way too embarrassed to talk to my parents about this, but I can't go and see a doctor without using their insurance cards. Lately it burns really bad whenever I pee or finish masturbating. My penis is kinda red and splotchy. I looked online to see what it could be and after reading several pages I'm convinced that I'm dying of penile cancer. Please tell me I'm wrong!

A. *That's a pretty big assumption you're making there about your diagnosis. Sure, it can be tempting to look online for everything. There are so many different forums with answers given by people, even doctors, and if you look at any of them for too long you're probably going to reach the conclusion that you're dying of something. However, it's a big leap for you to self-determine a fatal illness. It could just be a bladder infection or an STI, but the only way you're going to know, and stop the burning, is to see a real, living, non-zombie, non-computer-generated physician. If you're that horrified to talk to your parents, try to locate a confidential clinic in your area. Some of them are even free.*

Q. If I give oral sex to a guy but he doesn't cum in my mouth, I'm safe from disease, right?

A. As stated earlier in the chapter, certain STIs are carried in bodily fluids like semen. It is rare to contract these types of STIs through oral sex, but since the tissues in your mouth are a mucus membrane, they are more receptive to infection than regular skin, and an STI can potentially be transmitted. Other STIs, like herpes, are transmitted skin-to-skin (like from penis/vaginal skin to mouth skin), and these can be transmitted via oral sex more easily. So, by simply putting a penis in your mouth, you are putting yourself at some risk. While most doctors agree that unprotected oral sex is less risky than unprotected vaginal and anal sex, you'll still want to be safe and consider using a condom during oral sex, especially if you don't know your partner's sexual history.

THERE ARE NO STUPID QUESTIONS — EXCEPT FOR THIS ONE

Q. I am really mad at my ex for breaking up with me and then still showing up whenever he wants some action. What is the best STI that I can get quickly and give to him?

CHAPTER 8

BIRTH CONTROL

The Art of *Not* Making Babies

If you are having vaginal sex, you obviously know that it's a good way to get pregnant. In fact, it's the only way to get pregnant. And if you are a teenager, we strongly advise against getting pregnant (even if you happen to think it's a great idea).

The only way to completely prevent pregnancy is, obviously, to not have sex. But if you do have sex, using protection will massively narrow the chances of pregnancy. To be extra safe, many doctors even suggest you use two forms of birth control. Being so careful may seem like a drag, but it's a whole lot easier than dealing with an unwanted pregnancy.

EFFECTIVE FORMS OF BIRTH CONTROL

You read about how you get pregnant in Chapter 1, or maybe you just already knew. It's pretty basic stuff: The sperm makes its way to the egg, fertilizes it, and bam! — you or your partner is pregnant. So your task, as a sexually active person, is to prevent that sperm from ever fertilizing that egg. This is why you must always, always use birth control. There are many forms of birth control, but the two main acceptable categories of birth control are barrier methods and hormonal methods. Many people choose to use one primary form of birth control and one backup.

1. BARRIER METHODS

These types of birth control physically stop sperm from getting to eggs and include the following:

MALE CONDOM

WHAT IT IS: A latex or polyurethane tube that rolls on over a penis. The male condom is what most people are talking about when they say "a condom" and is a great primary form of birth control.

EFFECTIVENESS: Typically 85 percent.

FEMALE CONDOM

WHAT IT IS: A polyurethane tube with a ring at either end. It's inserted into the vagina and the frame ring is visible outside of the girl. It can be inserted up to eight hours before sex. This type of condom was invented to give a woman the chance to be responsible for bringing her own protection along, although women can also just bring a male condom and ask the guy to put it on. Because of the whole insertion element, the female condom never really took off. And the major disadvantage is that it's not as effective as the male condom in preventing pregnancy.

EFFECTIVENESS: Typically 79 percent.

MORE ABOUT BARRIER METHODS

Female condoms and diaphragms are not as commonly used as male condoms because they involve inserting things very deep into the vagina. And, as this is usually done directly before having sex, by the time you get it up there, you may no longer be interested in getting busy. Diaphragms also need to be custom fitted for you by a doctor (like being fitted for a retainer, only it's in your vagina instead of your mouth).

You can't use a male and female condom together (they would just rub against each other and break, providing zero percent protection), but you can use a diaphragm as a backup form to the male condom if you and your doctor decide that is best.

While you need to get diaphragms at the doctor, you can get condoms at the drugstore, no matter how old you are and regardless of what people say. Sure, some people would rather sell you candy and soda than see you actually take care of your body, but they were raised in a very different time and probably had to churn their own butter or something, so try to ignore them.

HOW EFFECTIVE IS IT?

The rates of effectiveness given here are based on typical use of the birth control method. "Typical use" takes into account the number of times a condom breaks or a birth control pill is missed. If you use your birth control perfectly every single time, the effectiveness of the birth control increases. For example, condoms are 98 percent effective if they are used the right way every time; but because people make mistakes or have slip-ups when using them, they are generally about 85 percent effective in preventing pregnancy. Birth control pills are 99.7 percent effective when used perfectly, but because people often forget one or take them at the wrong time, it winds up being more like 92 percent.

There isn't one method of birth control that is 100 percent effective, so it is smart to use two different types at the same time. And remember: The most effective forms of birth control are the ones you'll remember to use and use correctly.

WHY CONDOMS RULE

The best primary form of birth control is the one already recommended for preventing disease: a condom. Here's why:

- Kind of like a 2-in-1 shampoo and conditioner it protects against pregnancy and disease, so you can think of it as multi-tasking for your body.
- Other than remembering to carry one, you don't need to think about it beforehand — you just put it on and get to it.
- It has no side effects, short or long term.
- It's really effective when used perfectly every time.
- It's easy to buy.

To find out more about different kinds of condoms and how to put them on, turn back to pages 107-108.

2. HORMONAL METHODS

This is a method of birth control that involves a girl taking synthetic hormones like progestin and estrogen, which hormonally change the environment of the ovaries and therefore stop the girl from ovulating (releasing that monthly egg). There are various forms of these.

THE BIRTH CONTROL PILL

WHAT IT IS: A daily hormone pill you swallow. Some of them are taken for three weeks on, one week off; others are taken every day of the month. It is very important to take the pill at the same time every day, preferably pairing it with an activity like eating dinner or going to bed, as opposed to sometime between first period math class and fifth period PE. If you miss a pill, there are rules for when you should take the next one, and for whether or not you are still protected by the pill, so read the instructions carefully.

EFFECTIVENESS: Typically 92 percent.

THE PATCH

WHAT IT IS: A sticky, tan-colored patch that you wear on your skin and change weekly. It looks like a bandage or a nicotine patch, and it discharges hormones into your body through the skin. You can place it somewhere normally covered with clothing if you want to be discreet, or you can put it on your forearm and let the world know that you love being in charge of your birth control!

EFFECTIVENESS: Typically 92 percent.

THE RING

WHAT IT IS: A rubbery ring that you insert into your vagina. It discharges hormones into your body through the vagina and is effective for three weeks at a time. (The week you take it out is when you get your period.) It's good if you are one of those people who forget to take the pill daily, but you'll still need to use a good system that will help you remember when to change the ring. It's also not for those who are squeamish about putting their fingers inside themselves since it involves really sticking a hand up there to get it in properly and to take it out.

EFFECTIVENESS: Typically 92 percent.

THE SHOT (DEPO-PROVERA)

WHAT IT IS: A hormone shot administered by a doctor that is effective for three months. The shot is usually given in the arm or butt meat and doesn't hurt more than a normal shot. It certainly hurts less than childbirth.

EFFECTIVENESS: Typically 97 percent.

THE HORMONAL IUD

WHAT IT IS: A T-shaped plastic device inserted by a doctor into the uterus through the cervix that releases hormones into the body. It works for as long as it is inside.

EFFECTIVENESS: Typically 99 percent.

NOTE: There is also an older, non-hormonal copper IUD that works by sending signals to the sperm that affect its swimming ability. It's just as effective as the hormonal one.

MORE ABOUT HORMONAL METHODS

Remember that hormonal methods, while very good forms of birth control, do not protect against disease at all. They are best used as a backup to prevent pregnancy in case the condom breaks. If you use a hormonal method, don't just go stealing your mom's pills. Talk to a doctor about which method is best for you and get a prescription.

SIDE EFFECTS OF HORMONAL METHODS

For some people, the pill is a walk in the park. For others, taking hormones can have side effects, like weight gain, moodiness, skin changes, hair growing in new places, and even major menstrual changes. For anyone who smokes cigarettes, which isn't a good idea, using the pill can increase the risk of getting random blood clots, so no one should mix the pill and smoking. In addition to more minor side effects, hormonal methods can also be associated with an increased risk of things like stroke and heart attack, though that is rare. Just as you would before taking any other medication, you'll need to check with a doctor to figure out what's best and safest for your body.

For some girls, the side effects go away after the body adapts; for others, the mood changes are so severe that you don't need birth control because you bite your boyfriend's head off anytime he comes near.

Some side effects of the pill can also be good ones. Since the pill is designed to regulate hormones and stop ovulation, periods may be shorter, lighter, and less crampy than before. Some people even take the pill to help clear up acne. Talk to a doctor about all of this and see what's best for your bod and situation.

NON-RECOMMENDED FORMS OF BIRTH CONTROL

There are other forms of supposed birth control out there, but we don't recommend using them. In case you are curious about them, here's some more information.

SPERMICIDAL METHODS

Spermicide (sperm "killer") is a chemical compound, which generally contains Nonoxynol-9, a chemical that damages sperm. When used alone, it is less than 75 percent effective in preventing pregnancy, which is too much of a crap shoot. It can also be irritating to the genitals.

Sometimes, people use it to boost the effectiveness of a condom or diaphragm, which it can, but some studies have shown that this chemical may cause lesions in the vaginal and anal walls for some people, which can increase the risk of catching HIV and other STIs. So if you want to protect yourself against disease (which you do), you may want to opt for the condoms without Nonoxynol 9. If you are considering a diaphragm (see page 120), which only works with spermicide, ask your doctor what he or she thinks is best.

RHYTHM METHOD

This method does not involve drumming or dancing. Rather, it's all about keeping track of which days you are most likely to ovulate, and not having sex on those days. This is one of the least effective forms of birth control for adults and it is even less effective for teenagers, as your bodies are not yet regulated enough for you to know exactly when you will be ovulating. It really doesn't protect against pregnancy, and it definitely does not protect against STIs.

WITHDRAWAL METHOD

Another good name for this is the Don't Be Stupid Method. This method is simply pulling the penis out of the vagina before the dude has an orgasm. It is like asking the universe to give you a baby. For one, the boy

EMERGENCY CONTRACEPTION: PLAN B

Also known as the Morning After Pill, emergency contraception is not for when your house is on fire or an earthquake strikes — it is a method of birth control to be used when your first methods fail. Let's say the condom broke last night and you forgot to take your birth control pill two days ago and you want to make sure you don't risk pregnancy — that's when you take Plan B. Plan B is not an abortion pill, and it doesn't work if you are already pregnant. It contains the same hormones as birth control pills but the dosage is higher. It has to be taken within 72 hours of when you had the unprotected sex, and it can (but doesn't always) have some pretty bad side effects like heavy cramping, nausea, diarrhea, and headaches. But most people think those side effects are better than getting pregnant. Plan B should not be considered your regular birth control. It is for emergencies only. If you take it within 72 hours, it is 89 percent effective at preventing ovulation or interfering with the sperm fertilizing the egg. If you take it within 24 hours, it's 95 percent effective.

If you are 17, you can purchase emergency contraception at your local drugstore without a prescription. If you are under 17 you have to get a prescription from a doctor. In some states you can get confidential services at Planned Parenthood, which also sells Plan B. Some states require your parents' permission to receive services. Because those laws change frequently, you should call your local Planned Parenthood or use the national number on page 184 to ask if someone there can help you.

needs to be extra sure he can pull out in time. (Yeah, right.) And then there is the issue of pre-cum. Pre-cum (pre-ejaculatory fluid) is a small amount of fluid that may come out of the penis sometime between arousal and ejaculation (see more on page 74), and it may contain left-over sperm from the last time the boy masturbated or had sex, which means there's a chance that this left-over sperm can get a girl pregnant. Like the rhythm method, the withdrawal method is just not a safe, smart way to have sex.

UH, OH, I'M PREGNANT

If you totally failed with the contraception thing and you find that you are pregnant, don't bang your head against the wall. You are going to need your head in full working order so that you can deal with this new situation.

The first thing you need to figure out is what you are going to do. And you need to figure it out fairly quickly because you have a rapidly multiplying bunch of cells inside you and they are on their way to becoming a baby.

If your boyfriend or the baby's father is someone you trust, you can talk to him as you make your decision. This is a very big deal and you need other people around to help you sort through the feelings you will have. Close friends and family can be amazing supports, and so can some parents. Just be sure that you think this through and decide what will be best for you and the baby instead of letting other people pressure you into what they think is right.

There are three options for you to consider:

- abortion
- adoption
- raising the baby yourself

None of these choices are perfect or easy to deal with, but you will live through this just fine if you keep your wits about you.

ABORTION

An abortion is when you choose to terminate your pregnancy. If you decide to do this, it's best to do it as early as possible in your pregnancy.

The Abortion Pill (Medical Abortion): The abortion pill must be taken within nine weeks from your last period and needs to be prescribed by a physician who follows up with you in two to three weeks. The abortion pill is actually two pills taken within three days of each other. The first pill has hormones in it that stop your body from producing baby hormones, and the second pill is a medication that causes your body to expel the embryo. It is like having a very heavy period.

Common names for the abortion pill are Mifeprex, Mifepristone, and RU-486. (It is NOT the same thing as Plan B, which must be taken within 72 hours of unprotected sex (as mentioned on page 125). It's somewhat controversial and not available to teens in all states.

Abortion at a Clinic (Surgical Abortion): If you are going to have a surgical abortion, it's best to do it within 12 weeks from your last period. After that, the procedure gets more complicated.

Most surgical abortions work like this: Before the actual abortion, you will take some time to talk with the doctor and discuss your medical history, have a physical exam (this may include an ultrasound), and then read and sign papers.

To start the procedure, you'll first be offered pain or sedation medication. Then the doctor inserts a speculum into the vagina to gain access into the cervix and the uterus. The doctor may use medication or other instruments to dilate (open) your cervix a little bit, and then will insert a tube that gently sucks out the fertilized egg and all of the pregnancy tissue. Sometimes another instrument is used to gently remove any tissue that might be left behind. There is usually a recovery period of about an hour, and you're given antibiotics to prevent infection.

Medical abortion must be done by a doctor. You can have it done by your gynecologist, if he/she performs abortions, or you can go to a clinic like Planned Parenthood. Abortions can be costly and are not always covered by health insurance, unless the reason you are aborting is medical (such as the baby is not developing right or your health is at risk). One way or another, you should check with your insurance company.

Abortions can also be emotionally traumatic. While some girls don't feel a lot of sadness — or any at all — about having an abortion, others feel a whole range of emotions about the experience. To help deal with both the emotional and financial aspects of the procedure, it's best to have a family member or good, trustworthy friend to help you during this time. There is a list of resources on pages 184–185, if you feel like you want to talk to someone else.

Abortion has been legal in the US only since 1973. Many people still feel that abortion should be illegal (they say that it kills another human being), and if you choose to have an abortion, you may find these anti-abortion people protesting outside the clinic. Remember that it is your body and your decision, and don't let anyone scare you into making a choice that is not wholly your own.

The laws that tell us whether a teenager can have an abortion without parental consent vary from state to state. Call your local Planned Parenthood to find out what your options and rights are.

ADOPTION

Adoption is when you actually have the baby but then give it to someone else after he or she is born. It is a special thing to do for a family, but the process itself can be difficult. Your decision to give up your baby may seem pretty straighforward initially and then, as the pregnancy goes on, you may feel more attached to the baby. This is why adoption is a legal process that typically begins before the baby is born but isn't completed until after the birth.

If you pick this route, you'll also need to think about what terms you want around the adoption. You may opt for an open adoption, in which you either regularly see the baby, get pictures only once a year, or just keep your information updated so that if the child ever wants to, he or she will know how to contact you. You can also opt for a closed adoption, in which you keep your identity a secret because you don't want contact in the future. Do some research to make sure you select the right adoption agency for you.

Whatever type of adoption you decide on, make sure you have people to help you get through the nine months of pregnancy, and find a support group for young mothers who are giving (or have already given) their

CAN I GET PREGNANT ON MY PERIOD?

The short answer is yes. But it's not that likely. When your body releases its monthly egg to a fallopian tube, the egg will live for up to two days and sperm can live for several days. So you can get pregnant from sperm that is hanging around before you ovulate and also afterward. Most women ovulate in the middle of their cycle (right between periods), but some ovulate closer to the time of menstruation, especially teens who still don't have regular period cycles. So, technically, you could get pregnant from having sex during your period if you ovulate close enough to it.

Having sex while on your period may also increase the chance of contracting or spreading an STI because of the extra bodily fluids present. So use both STI and birth control protection, even while on your period.

baby up for adoption. Those people need to talk to you as much as you need to talk to them.

KEEPING YOUR BABY

This is probably the hardest road of all: financially, emotionally, and socially. Being a parent can be a very cool thing, but your entire world is going to change forever. Right now, your life is all about you. Any money in your pocket or bank account is for you alone. Once a baby is a part of your life, everything is about the baby. If you decide to keep and raise this child, set up a support system right away. Draft a financial plan to make sure you will be able to provide for your child. This should include the baby's father (it's his responsibility, too, and even if he doesn't want to be in the baby's life, he still has a financial responsibility). Strengthen your relationships with friends and relatives you can call on for help, and find a local parenting group that can guide you through trying times.

BIRTH CONTROL MYTHS

We've come a long way since people believed that having sex standing up on a full moon was an effective form of birth control. So, what else isn't true?

Here are some of the top birth control myths debunked.

- Washing out the vagina or douching after sex does not prevent baby-making. And douching with weird things (cola, perfume, Gatorade, bleach) to try to induce an abortion is ineffective and even dangerous. So don't try it.
- Toothpaste is not a spermicide.
- Plastic wrap and rubber gloves are not replacements for condoms.
- You can get pregnant the first time you have sex.
- It is not effective to throw yourself down stairs, or onto the ground, or inflict physical trauma to yourself to cause an at-home abortion. You will most likely stay pregnant and cause more harm than good.
- Neither hopping up and down after you have sex nor having sex standing up will stop the sperm from getting to your eggs. Gravity is no match for tenacious sperm.
- Being stoned or intoxicated will not make a guy infertile. If some guy tells you that he's smoked enough pot or eaten enough marijuana seeds to make his semen sterile, tell him you're not stoned enough to believe that and that he needs to put on a condom (or maybe you should put your clothes on and leave, because who would want to do it with a guy like that anyway). •

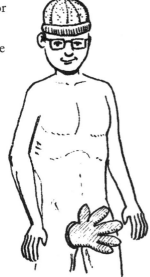

Q & A

Q. I asked my parents if I could start taking the pill, and they said no way. I am not having sex yet, but I know that I want to and I would rather be safe about it before it happens. Even if they tell me no, I'm going to have sex, so how can I get them to support my choice and let me get on birth control?

A. First of all, remember that if you decide to have sex, you need to also take precautions to protect against disease by using condoms, as the birth control pill does not protect against disease. You don't need your parents' permission to get condoms.

In terms of your parents not allowing you to take the pill, well … who knows why they are doing that. Maybe they had a bad experience with the pill. Maybe they believe that if they stop you from taking the pill, they'll stop you from losing your virginity. You made a very responsible choice to explore birth control options and to try to talk openly to your parents about sex. Unfortunately, some parents don't really deal well with talking to their kids about sex.

You don't actually need your parents' permission to be on birth control in most states in the US. If you don't have a strong enough relationship with your family doctor to ask for a prescription for birth control pills, you can find your local Planned Parenthood office and meet with a doctor there to get confidential services.

Also, even if your parents seem to be shutting you down, keep trying to communicate with them. They may have concerns you don't know about — ask them what they are instead of making assumptions. The more you are able to speak and listen to each other, the better your relationship will be. And if they really seem disinterested and inflexible regarding your point of view, remember that you won't be living at home forever.

Q. My boyfriend told me that he is clean and that he doesn't like to use condoms because it doesn't feel the same when we have sex. Since he told me he is clean, is it OK for me to just take the pill?

A. Your boyfriend is right. Sex with condoms feels different. And since your boyfriend knows what the difference feels like, that means he has had unprotected sex before, which is something to be concerned about.

It doesn't mean much if a person professes to be clean. After all, some STIs don't present any noticeable symptoms in some people, in which case those people don't always know they are infected. Therefore, you should always use a condom. And even if your boyfriend and you totally trust each other and also get tested for every STI, there is still the matter of birth control. Even if you are on the pill, there is a chance it could fail.

Q. I am pregnant, and there is no way I am ready to take care of a baby. I have heard that abortions can make it so that I am unable to have a baby later on and that they cost a lot. Is this true?

A. First of all, it is not true that having an abortion will leave you unable to have children in the future. Until relatively recently, women in the US could not legally have an abortion, but women continued to have them anyway — and not in safe and clean medical facilities by doctors. These "back alley abortions" caused women to get ill and would sometimes lead to infections that would result in infertility because the women were too afraid to see a doctor. We live in a different time now, and an abortion is a safe procedure.

Having one can be expensive, though. Abortions done in the early stages of pregnancy can cost anywhere from $300 to $1,000, depending on factors like where you live, how far along you are in the pregnancy, and if your insurance will cover any of the cost. Some clinics and states will assist financially with loans or offer pay scales based on your income. While the person who got you pregnant is legally required to support the baby if you have it, he is not legally required to help you pay for an abortion. However, it is the right thing for him to do, if that's the decision you make, and it will cost him a lot less than 18 years of child support.

Q. I have heard that if you give up a baby for adoption and then you have another baby when you are older you have to go to court to prove you can take care of your baby. I really want to be a mother one day, just not right now. Will I lose my chance?

A. This is all just a myth. There are no laws anywhere at all that say a woman who has given up her child for adoption needs to prove anything in the future about her ability to care for another child. Make your decision based on what feels right to you, and rest assured that your day for motherhood will come.

Q. How do I get a pregnancy test?

A. Pregnancy tests are sold at the drugstore. They are often kept behind the counter, but that doesn't mean you need some sort of special note from God to get one. It's just that people steal them a lot. There is a wide variety of tests, but they are all basically the same and, nowadays, highly accurate. If you are worried at all about your ability to pee on something properly, buy one of those boxes with more than one test inside. Once you get the test, it is really important that you follow the directions.

You can also go to a doctor, clinic, or place like Planned Parenthood to be tested. It will probably cost more, but the advantage is that if you are pregnant you'll have a professional there to calmly lay out your options for you. Be wary, however, of suspicious phone book ads for places called "crisis pregnancy centers" that offer free pregnancy tests. These places can sometimes be really creepy, and your "free" pregnancy test may come along with a two-hour lecture and video about aborted babies. Many women describe being harassed, intimidated, and given blatantly false information at these places — hardly what you need at such a sensitive time.

Q. Can I get pregnant if my boyfriend and I are just fooling around naked and his penis is close to my vagina?

A. If you are naked together and rubbing your vagina and penis together and he has an orgasm near the opening of your vagina, then it is technically possible for his semen to get into your vagina and for you to get pregnant. But, unless the penis actually enters the vagina, it is pretty unlikely. And if he doesn't ejaculate, even if there is some pre-cum (see page 74), it is even less likely. So if you did this, he probably didn't get you pregnant. That being said, it's not the smartest thing to do because as long as your sexual organs are touching, you are risking picking up an STI.

CHAPTER 9

DATING AND RELATIONSHIPS

What's Sex Got to Do With It?

Sex does affect relationships, and relationships affect sex. There's no way around it. Although some people decide that they are not going to have relationships or sex when they are in high school because they don't want to get distracted from all of the other things in their lives, many others will have some kind of relationship with someone at some point. Whatever types of relationships you get yourself into during your teen years, from the two-day fling to the year-long romance, questions about sex will come up and decisions will need to be made. Even the decision not to have sex is a decision about sex.

MODERN ROMANCE

If you are thinking about having sex, then presumably you are already dating, whether it's by hanging out in groups or seeing people one-on-one. Times have changed from the days when people went to school, dated one person, got married, and had babies, who would then go to school, date one person, and continue the cycle. These days, there are categories and subcategories of types of relationships that are pretty much defined by the social scene in your high school. Here is a basic of the definitions:

- Dating: You are just starting to get to know each other, and it's still pretty casual.
- Going out: It's exclusive. You aren't dating anyone else.
- Hooking up: You're only getting physical with that person and not necessarily having any other kind of relationship.
- Friends with benefits: You and a friend hook up on a regular basis but don't want to have a relationship.

Whatever kind of relationship you find yourself in, be sure that you and your partner are on the same page about what that relationship is.

OMG! ONLINE DATING!

Technology gets extra points for improving the chances of people finding each other. Who knew there was someone out there who loves turtles as much as you do? The trouble with online dating is that you have no way of completely knowing if someone is as great as he or she claims. If you are hanging in a chat room you may be talking to some old loser who wants to earn your trust so that he can bury you in his back yard (or masturbate when you send pics of yourself making cute kissy faces). Only time, phone calls, and eventually meeting face-to-face (in a heavily populated, well-lit area, with a couple of your friends in tow) will tell you if you've found true love or a true loser.

ARE YOU IN LOVE?

So, you met someone you think is just about the best thing that's come along since fruit-scented Magic Markers. A whole swarm of butterflies just landed in your stomach and you're sure it'll never leave. Every movie, poem, and song suddenly seems like it was written for you. It doesn't even have to be a love song. It can be a commercial for auto repair shops that reminds you that your special someone ... drives a car. You have turned into that annoying person who always talks about your boyfriend or girlfriend, and relates everything back to your relationship.

The word love gets used as often as a question mark, and it sometimes even feels like one. That said, teens often can be more passionate than adults and feel things more deeply (for better or for worse). So if you think you are in love after knowing someone five days, you very well might be. Just because the adults in your life may be making light of it and insisting that there is no way you could even know what love is yet doesn't mean that your love isn't the real thing. (You love your family, but they don't question that.) Of course, you could also just be infatuated or stuck in a codependent and unhealthy situation in which you both feel you will die without each other. Ultimately, you really need to think about what it is you are feeling.

Even if it is true love, you certainly can't let it take over your life. When you are really into someone, try to remind yourself that the other people in your life still need your time and attention. And don't make any hasty decisions, especially about sex, just because you feel all gooey inside for a new person. Tell yourself that if this is really love and not just a fleeting burst of hormones, it will be better to wait and get to know the person in every way you possibly can so that if you get physical you will have an even better experience.

MAKING A COMMITMENT

One definition for "being committed" is being put in an insane asylum — but it also means being in a faithful relationship where neither of you

UNREQUITED LOVE

This is one of the crappiest things there is — when you really want to be with someone and he or she doesn't want to be with you. It feels like a punch in your stomach instead of those butterflies flittering. There is nothing you can do to make someone want you.

Yes, it hurts, but don't panic. It won't feel like that forever. One day you'll find someone better and hotter and funnier who sees you for the awesome person you are. In the meantime, schedule lots of time with good friends and write some terrible poems that you can laugh at later.

date or sleep with other people. Crossing the line into commitment is a big step, but it can be a really awesome thing for your relationship. It means you have someone you can depend on in times of need (or just for a fun night out or help with algebra homework). But just because you're in a committed relationship doesn't mean you have to have sex, no matter what TV tells you. Plenty of people manage to have healthy relationships without jumping straight into bed together. And while some people do have sex without a relationship, doing it with someone you know and trust often leads to better sex because you feel safer and more comfortable.

Of course, commitments don't always last forever and commitment is not for everyone. If you suddenly find yourself very attracted to another person, that may be a sign that you're not happy with your relationship. However, some people find that even if they truly love the person they're with, they have the inclination to date or hook up with other people. If you are questioning whether commitment is right for you for whatever reason, the best solution, as always, is to discuss it with your partner. The worst thing to do in any relationship is to lie. (Posting an unflattering photo of your boyfriend or girlfriend online is a close second.)

WILL HAVING SEX CHANGE MY RELATIONSHIP?

Well, yes. It won't necessarily change it for better or worse, but it will change it. Sex often kicks a relationship up a notch, making it more serious. It's unavoidable. In many cases, it brings people closer together, which is great. Of course, if you start feeling like the relationship is getting too serious, you need to talk about this with your partner. (The fact that sex will intensify the relationship is also a good thing to think about before you actually have sex.)

Sometimes sex can change things in the opposite way, especially if it comes too soon. You may have had really intense feelings for the other person only to find that after sex you just feel awkward. This doesn't make you a bad person. Sometimes just the choice is bad for that given situation. Try to be mature about it, and talk things through. If you can't work it out you may choose to part ways. Just do it respectfully.

If you start having sex a lot and find that your friendship is now overshadowed by just making out and having sex, make it a point to disconnect your bodies long enough to do things together that involve clothing. Sometimes relationships fizzle out if there isn't substance beyond the bedroom. If the relationship is meant to last, you'll eventually find a balance between the sexual and nonsexual times you have with your partner.

BREAKING UP

All of a sudden every song ever written is about you again, but this time there is no soft-focus smile on your face when you are listening. A bad breakup can make you feel like you will never smile again. Nothing your friends say or do can make it feel better because they aren't inside of you, feeling how heavy everything is. Even though everyone has been there, each breakup is different, and the way you deal with it will be different each time.

IS IT OVER?

If you're at that point where the relationship you are in is feeling stale, hold off for a minute on breaking up. Think back to how you felt about that person when you got together and figure out what changed. If you are both mature enough to have dated, you are mature enough to talk about the relationship. If you can pinpoint what's bothering you, let your partner know (be kind!) and see if that helps address the problem. Perhaps nothing will help, but at least he or she won't be completely shocked when you decide it's over.

YOU'VE BEEN DUMPED

If you are the one who was broken up with, you may find yourself questioning if you have anything to offer. You could be angry with the other person or still be madly in love. If he or she was your "first," or even the second or third, the feeling could be even worse; you may feel like you shared an intimate piece of you but now you're alone. If the breakup comes right after having sex the first time, it can feel really bad — like all that person wanted from you was the sex. It is important that you remember that you made a choice that you thought was right at the time. You cannot undo any of it. But you can know that you are still a whole person and there are people who won't use you for sex.

No matter what, don't call them. Yes, at one time you two shared everything and you want to run back to the only person who cares about you and will listen — but put down the phone. Don't send that late-night email about how much you want to rekindle things. You can write an email (or, better yet, keep a journal of the different things you are thinking about), but don't send it! If your ex replies or doesn't reply it will only drag out the rotten feelings.

YOU ARE DOING THE DUMPING

If you are the person breaking things off, no matter how much you've come to dislike that person, have a little bit of respect for what he or she is about to go through. Always break up in person, not through text, email, or over the phone. Don't have your friends do it for you, and don't just avoid the person. Even if your now ex is getting hysterical, keep calm. You'll need to answer why this is happening, and you should try to make your reason as painless as possible.

And avoid contacting your ex, even if you are feeling just as bad about the breakup. The person you dumped is not your support system. Talk to your friends about it. They may not realize how crappy you are really feeling since you were the dumper.

AFTER IT'S OVER

After the breakup, you'll likely miss a whole bunch of things: your former partner's company, his or her laugh and hugs, and, possibly, the sex. This is only natural — after all, you had a strong connection and felt comfortable with each other. Feeling lonely can lead to "breakup sex," which means having sex with an ex without having a relationship in place. Breakup sex can feel good at that moment because you two have been missing each other, but the aftermath is often messy, because it makes you miss each other even more. It can even make you both feel angry and used. In general, breakup sex is not a great idea.

You might also be tempted to have a rebound fling, which is when you start hooking up with someone else too soon after your breakup in order to try to fill the void your partner left, boost your confidence, or show your ex that you're doing just fine. Sometimes a rebound can turn into a relationship, which is great. But lots of times, it won't work because you still have too many feelings for your ex. If possible, try to take some time between relationships so that you are clear on your feelings when you start a new relationship.

DEALING WITH AN ABUSIVE RELATIONSHIP

No one likes to think they'll ever wind up in an abusive relationship, but it happens to the best of us. If your partner puts you down, yells at you, tells you that you're fat, insists you do things you don't want to, or hits you, it's abuse. If your partner scares you into staying with him or her, isolates you from spending time with others, threatens you, or lies to friends and family in an effort to control you, that's also abuse. Unfortunately, if you're being abused, you might also be so mixed up about the abuse that you have trouble recognizing it. The person abusing you might even tell you that what he or she is doing is what you deserve. It's a good idea to listen to your gut, but also listen to the people around you who care about you. And in this situation there's only one thing to do: Get out.

You may feel like you can change your partner into the caring, thoughtful person you know is deep down inside of him or her, but you are not a doctor (yet), so leave the fixing to the therapists and start taking care of yourself. And if your partner tries to talk you into staying in the relationship, even telling you that you will never find anyone else who will want to be with you, stay strong. The abuse is your partner's issue, not yours. See page 185 for some numbers you can call if you find yourself in an abusive relationship.

Also, you might find that you're the abusive person in the relationship. Hopefully that's something you want to change about yourself, because you are capable of having all of the good things that come from a loving and honest connection. Sometimes you just need to deal with your own emotional junk before you'll be able to be a healthy partner. If you're the abuser, don't get stuck in that pattern. You deserve help, too, even though you might feel like you're a monster. You can use the resources on page 185 to find services, as well. •

Q & A

Q. I am totally in love with my girlfriend. She is perfect for me, and I want to be with her every second of every day. But my parents don't like her at all. They told me I am not allowed to date her, and they do things to make sure all my free time is taken up so I can't go to her house. They tried saying that the issue is that I am too young to date, but they didn't have trouble with my last two girlfriends. I'm not going to stop seeing her. How can I make them understand?

A. *Have you tried stomping your feet, yelling "But I love her!" and running to your room and slamming the door? (Just so you know, that rarely works.) Your parents will always think that they know what is best for you. Sometimes they are right, sometimes they aren't. You might want to consider what it is they don't like about your girlfriend to see if they might be on to something, but if you really don't agree, try to have a serious talk with them about trust. Tell them they should give you space to make choices, and making choices could mean making mistakes. In sitting down to calmly tell them that you are mature enough to stay on the right path, you make a huge step toward proving that maturity. One thing* *you could tell them is that it would be better for them to allow you to see this girl in their home than to have you sneaking around to do it. This way they could sort of oversee things. If they really are concerned that you are not ready to date, suggest that you have your girlfriend over for dinner or to spend time with all of you. Maybe that will give them a chance to see what you find so wonderful about this girl.*

Q. What do I do if my boyfriend forces me to have sex? Is that still considered rape if he's my boyfriend?

A. *Any time any person has sex with you and you have not agreed to it, it is rape. Whether it is a stranger, a first date, a relationship partner, or even a spouse, you have the right to say no, and the other person must respect that. If your boyfriend has forced you to have sex, even once, you need to break up with him. There is no "waiting for him to get help" or giving him one more chance. He does need help, but he needs to find a professional for that.*

You also have the option to report him to the police, but that can be a hard process. If you choose to do it, know that no matter what people say, it was not your fault and what he did was not OK. If you decide not to report him, at least make him accountable by telling him it was wrong and involve an adult you trust. If he's not held accountable in some way, he may do it again to someone else.

As for you, consider talking to a counselor or therapist about the experience. This will help you to eventually move past it. If you don't know of someone, see pages 184-185 for a list of resources.

Q. I am a lesbian and started dating this girl a few months ago, and she seemed to be really cool. But after a few weeks, she started getting obsessive and weird, doing things like reading my emails and getting jealous over nothing. I was

going to break it off after she freaked out and broke a bunch of my CDs, but she said she would kill herself. Sometimes she's wonderful, but the bad times are the worst I have ever seen. I care about her, but I have to find a way to make her stop freaking out, and I don't want to feel like I'm responsible for her staying alive.

A. *Do you hear that sound? It's the DANGER alarm. You're in a tricky situation here and no matter what happens things are going to be difficult. Based on what you've said, your girlfriend has a lot of serious issues that she needs to resolve. Without intending to, she is being emotionally abusive to you, and that is unacceptable.*

Your only options are to either push your girl to get professional help or break up with her. Even as she starts to get help, she'll have good days and bad. She'll need to be told that while you support her and want her to get better, you also have limits. She can't bully you, lash out in paranoia, invade your privacy, or threaten to harm herself. All of those things are deal breakers, and if she continues to behave this way, you should leave the relationship.

Loving someone with emotional problems is very difficult. The number one rule to remember is: You are not responsible for her decisions. If she decides to get help, that will be her decision; and if she decides to harm herself, that is also her decision. And nothing that you did drove her to it.

THERE ARE NO STUPID QUESTIONS — EXCEPT FOR THIS ONE

Q. This guy wrote a song about me, sent me a dozen roses, and recites poetry under my window. How can I tell if he likes me?

CHAPTER 10

KINKS, FANTASIES, AND FETISHES

Not Just in Your Imagination

So, now you know how to figure out if you're ready for sex, how to prepare yourself, and how to protect yourself. But sex isn't always that cut and dry. Some people like their sex straight up, others like a whole bunch of bells and whistles, and pretty much everyone has one special thing they like to do or think of when they're getting it on. Some sexual quirks are just built into us, and others we pick up along the way. So whether you like to role-play as waiter and cook, be covered in chocolate, or fondle a plushy panda while you get it on, you should know that it's all entirely normal. (Well, maybe not the panda thing.)

KINKS, FETISHES, AND FANTASIES

When it comes to classifying the strange stuff that turns us on, it usually comes down to a kink, fetish, or fantasy. Here's a breakdown of all three.

KINK

An activity that you're interested in trying or are likely to try when you feel comfortable with your sexual partner. Some common examples of kinks are spanking, tying each other up, role- playing, or wearing costumes. A less common, but totally valid, kink might be pinching during sex.

FETISH

An object, item of clothing, or part of the body that, when present, gets you sexually excited. Some common examples of fetishes are high heels and leather. Of course, anything can be a fetish, even noses. The spectrum is so wide, it can go from a Brad fetish (you simply cannot have an orgasm unless someone named Brad is involved) to mysophilia (you get aroused by soiled or dirty material) to fantasizing about women wearing seatbelts (a very safe-sex fantasy).

SEXUAL FANTASY

This is a situation that you like to think about or play out during sex. Some people fantasize about being dominated or dominating a partner, having sex with a stranger, having sex with a teacher or boss, or having sex in public. Some even fantasize about pretending to be animals while they have sex. A fantasy can remain in your head forever, or, if it's safe, legal, and no actual animals (or people) are harmed, it can be enacted in a role-play (such as, if you have a fantasy about having sex with a pilot, you could ask your partner to put on some flying goggles and speak to you in a soothing tone about the altitude). That being said, not all fantasies are meant to be acted out. Some are just meant to be imagined. For instance, if you find that you like to think about getting trampled by an entire football team while having sex, you probably wouldn't want to actually act that out.

SAFETY FIRST!

You can never be too safe, so remember to wear condoms, stay sober during sex, and look both ways before crossing the street (on the way over to your partner's house). In the case of kinks, fetishes, and sexual fantasies, you have one more safety issue: If you are trying things with your partner that can cause discomfort or even pain, the two of you need to establish a word that either of you can use when you want things to stop. The word should be something extremely removed from sex. A fine example for this is the word appetizer, (unless your fetish is about waiters). Steer away from using the words no or stop or even ouch because those could be misconstrued as a part of the game.

TO PLAY OR NOT TO PLAY?

If your boyfriend or girlfriend is all about trying things that make you feel sick to your stomach, express how you feel and why. It is perfectly

WHAT IS BDSM

BDSM, which stands for the really long acronym of Bondage and Discipline, Dominance and Submission, and Sadism and Masochism, is when two people decide to commit to a safe yet unconventional sexual relationship in which one person dominates the other. It can involve a lot of different forms of sexual expression, including things like leather, whips, contracts, collar-wearing, and spanking. It's a big decision that is made by two consenting adults and, in general, is not appropriate for teens.

AND YOU THOUGHT YOU WERE STRANGE ...

There is a fetish, fantasy, or kink for just about everything you could think of. Next time you feel like you are weird in the things you think are sexual, read over this list of some of the more unusual turn-ons that exist in our wild and wonderful universe.

- Cake farting. This one is just what it sounds like. There are people out there who get really turned on by watching a person fart. On a cake.
- Balloon fetishists. These people like to watch others inflate, deflate, and even pop balloons. Just goes to show that what makes babies cry can be sexy to some people.
- Scat and golden showers. Some people like to be peed and even pooped on.
- Dinner crushing: For this one, one person has the other cook dinner for them, then step on it or otherwise crush it with their naked body. The person watching then has to eat the crushed dinner. (This one must come from too many ruined meal times as a child.)

Of course, these are a bit extreme. But it's just to say that anything goes when it comes to what turns people on.

OK to say no to something you have no interest in doing, even if you have already started playing along. Then again, you might find that you like to do things he or she suggested after you've tried them. Find a line between calling your partner a weirdo and maintaining respect for yourself. And never do something you think is unsafe or that makes you feel bad about yourself.

THE DEAL WITH PORN

Some people like to look at pictures or movies of people having sex. This is called pornography, or porn. There's a lot of stigma about porn being bad for you, that it will warp your sexual perspective or turn you into a creep, but that's not necessarily the case. Looking at porn can be a healthy habit as long as you are not overusing it (watching it all the time). Also, although the people making porn are real people doing their job, it is important to understand that your partner is probably not going to look that buff or skinny (and be so waxed and hair-free!). (A lot of plastic surgery, makeup, and retouching goes into making mainstream porn actors look the way they do, and you should love your partner's body for the way that it looks naturally.)

There's porn for every occasion and fetish, but remember that if you're under 18, and in some states 21, it's illegal for you to look at it. So you may not be able to get your hands on any nudey pics until you're of age. And if you do, just know you can get busted for it.

REMEMBER THAT IT'S A GAME!

Before you engage in any kind of kink or fetish behavior with your boyfriend or girlfriend, there are a couple of things to consider. Most important, make sure you have a good, solid basis of mutual respect in your relationship, and that both of you have a strong sense of self-respect. Make sure you will be able to communicate openly with your partner. No one should ever do anything that feels demoralizing in any kind of way. This is all for fun.

Also, don't use these games to try to cope with emotional issues from your childhood (for instance, asking someone to inflict pain upon you as a way of forgetting or trying to work out your feelings around having been abused). Kinky behavior won't erase your past, so make sure you and your relationship are emotionally stable before reaching for the leather or wacky chicken suit.

THE INTERNET!

Oh, the magical playground of anyone with access to a computer and button-pushing skills. The internet is our friend because it shows us how very many people are similar to us, but beware: Those over-18 sites tell you to go away and find something else to do for a reason. It is not only illegal for you to look at porn online and totally illegal for people to look at you naked anywhere, but it's also impossible to trust anonymous avatars on sex sites. You don't want to end up being stalked by some gross person or, worse, dead in some creep's crawl space. Stay away from anything that involves sex on the internet.

More important, porn is not for teens to make. For the sake of all that is sacred in this world, don't videotape yourself doing anything sexual. Don't take pictures or even have your really cool friend from art class paint a portrait. Remember that it is called the "adult entertainment" industry because people under 18 are not allowed to be a part of it. Not only could you wind up in jail, but your ability to get into college or find a job later in life could be hurt if colleges or employers find out about it. Besides which, you really don't want to be tomorrow's top story on the morning news: "New teen sex tape!" Do yourself a favor and stay out of the porn world.

OK, SO WHAT'S EROTICA?

Erotica is a story in a book or magazine that tells about sexy things happening. People like it because it can be fun to read other people's fantasies. Sometimes they think of themselves within those sexual situations, or just find it funny. (You are allowed to laugh.)

If you are a writer by nature and have some sexy story ideas of your own, you could write your own erotica. But beware: You are a teen and that means you have no privacy no matter how locked you think your door is. If you write this stuff but don't want your parents to find it and

have a heart attack from thinking you are writing about things you have done personally, stash your stories away in a good, safe place. You cannot publish these stories quite yet because even if they aren't autobiographical, they're considered a type of pornography, and, as you know by now, you have to be at least 18 for that. But writing about your fantasies is a good outlet, especially if those fantasies are ones you don't really want to act out — now or ever. •

Q & A

Q. My girlfriend says she wants me to tie her up during sex. Why does she want me to do that? And what should I do?

A. We're all wired differently, and we all like different things for different reasons. So it's hard to say why she wants you to do that. The easiest thing to do would be to ask her. If you decide you are up for it, remember that safety is the primary concern above all else. To keep it safe, one should use magician's rope or hemp rope, either of which is stretchy, unties easily, and is less likely to give rope burn. Use only simple-to-tie knots that come out easily, like reef knots; never, ever tie rope around someone's neck (that is very dangerous), and check in periodically to make sure that your girlfriend is still cool with being tied up. (If she isn't, obviously, untie her!)

Q. My boyfriend likes student–teacher role-plays and I'm worried that this comes from an obsession with a real teacher. Should I be worried, or are fantasies not related to real life?

A. While it's possible that your boyfriend's fantasies have a basis in real life, it's more likely that he's just generally turned on by the idea of an older experienced woman teaching him, a younger man, the joys of sex. This is a fairly common fantasy, just as it is with girls to fantasize about an older man. It will only harm your relationship if you get all paranoid that your boy is going to start cruising for old ladies. Fantasies are just that — sexual imagination running to wherever our mind takes us. And while there may be some elements from the real world from time to time, most people don't try to make those fantasies happen in real life. If you don't want to take part in the student-teacher role-play, why not suggest something that you fantasize about? Or maybe it's possible to find a middle ground in which both of your fantasies are taken care of.

Q. I like the idea of a boy totally dominating me, but my boyfriend is too nice. He's afraid that he'll say something wrong or hurt me, but I really don't care. If I give him pointers I don't think it will excite me as much, because I'll be showing him how to be dominant and I think that will ruin it for me. Is there any way I can make him take control?

A. Your boyfriend has likely been brought up being told that he should respect women, which is a great thing and probably makes him a great boyfriend. Of course, it doesn't really help if you're asking him to dominate you sexually. It sounds like this is a new and scary thing for your boyfriend to be experiencing, so he's completely out of his realm. Although telling him exactly what to do may ruin the experience for you, it may be worthwhile to simply inform him why you want him to dominate you and why this is so important to you. You could also try writing down scenarios, making sure to include things that your fantasy dominant man says and does to you.

It may also be that he feels that saying certain things to you may sound silly, and that if he says something wrong you may laugh at him. Next time he tries to take control, make sure you react so he knows when he's doing or saying the right thing, and his confidence will soar.

Of course, he may just not be into it. Maybe, like you, he prefers it if someone else takes charge. In that case, if this is really important to you, you might need to call it quits and find someone more suited to your interests.

Q. My boyfriend keeps making jokes about watersports. What is he talking about?

A. "Watersports" is basically peeing on your partner before or after sex, which some people report being really into. Urine (from a healthy person) is actually sterile, so having it come in contact with your skin is not really that unsanitary. You should know, however, that you can't drink it because of the salt and mineral content, and some people get rashes when it comes into contact with their skin.

THERE ARE NO STUPID QUESTIONS — EXCEPT FOR THIS ONE

Q. I really like having sex. Is that a fetish?

CHAPTER 11

COMMUNICATING ABOUT SEX

Mouths Are Also For Talking

There are songs, blogs, websites, and books about it. It seems you can't go an entire day without it coming up in the news or on a television show. Sex is everywhere, and everyone has something to say about it. You probably have a thing or two to say, as well. And even though you've just read a whole book on the topic, you probably still have plenty of questions.

Despite it being less than comfortable at times, it is really important that you and your friends start talking about sex and keep talking about it. Practice now. Try yelling out, "Sex! Sex! Sex!" This is especially a good idea if you are in a library. Librarians secretly love noise. And sex.

Seriously, communicating about sex can help you avoid (and cope with) major issues like pregnancy, STIs, and freaking out when your body is doing something you don't understand. So start talking, and keep talking.

TALKING TO YOUR PARTNER

We're all taught fairly young to be polite. Thank goodness. (See? Mention politeness and you end up thanking someone or something.) Sometimes, however, manners cause trouble, like when you can't tell whether someone's being honest or just sugarcoating things. This happens with some subjects more than others, and sex and relationships are both pretty complicated topics for all involved. Even if you feel one way one day, that could change the next. It is best to openly discuss your feelings with your significant other or the person you are hooking up with.

For instance, maybe you only want to have sex in a committed relationship, or you just want a hook-up, or you find that after finally having sex, you are no longer interested in spending forever (or the whole semester) together. It is far better to be honest about all of this. You can't expect someone to know where you are coming from if you don't speak up.

Also, if you are hooking up with someone and you start to have stronger feelings for that person, it can be scary expressing those feelings. You may stay quiet about it so that you don't say or do anything that might create a diversion. But remember that if you don't say anything, it is possible that your hook-up will never know, and you might lose out on a good thing.

Then there is the sex stuff. The more comfortable you get talking to people about all of the parts of you, the easier it will be to just say, "Hey, I'm on my period. We can either throw down some towels or wait till next week." You will also be more comfortable talking about safety, as well as the things you want to try and the things you don't enjoy.

Even if you are shy or not so good with words, you'll want to get a handle on communication. Practicing how to talk to a partner now will be really helpful down the line, as well. Adults spend all sorts of money on marriage or relationship counselors because they couldn't figure out how to discuss with each other what they need and want — or how they prefer to have the dishwasher loaded.

WITH FRIENDS LIKE THOSE, WHO NEEDS DOCTORS?

You may have friends who know an awful lot about sex, which is great because you can be open and expressive when talking about it with them without the fear of being judged, and you can also get some good information. But as much as your friends may think they know about everything, they may have a thing (or 12) wrong. So, always remember to follow up by getting important information from more reliable sources, like doctors or people listed in the Resources section at the back of the book (pages 184-185).

TALKING TO YOUR GOOD FRIENDS

These people are probably the easiest to talk to. Unlike your family, you chose them, so you must like them. With good friends, you can open up about all the things you feel nobody would understand — and you won't be judged. While adults are there to help you with really big deal things, your friends can support you in all things. They will also (hopefully) be honest with you when they see you getting into a situation that may be dangerous (like an abusive relationship). Your friends are the people you can always talk to, like when you are freaking out because your period is a day late or you can't have an orgasm when your girlfriend gives you oral sex.

And if you see your friends making bad choices, you will want to say something. Remember that just as important as what you say is how you say it. Even if you are right when you are telling your friend that she or he is partying too much, your friend may shut down completely if you seem to be coming from a place of disdain instead of a place of support.

TALKING TO YOUR PARENTS

It's great to educate yourself about sex, and that's what you're doing by reading this book. But what about educating your parents?

Your parents don't actually need you to educate them about the details

AND THAT'S WHEN YOUR DAD PUT HIS...

of sex. They've done it. That's how you're here. What your parents need to be educated about is what role sex is playing in your life. They don't know if you're doing it, or who you're doing it with, or how many of your friends are doing it. They don't know if you are being responsible about the way you are doing it. Unless you talk to your parents, they are pretty much in the dark about everything. The only thing they do know, and the thing that freaks them out, is that you are becoming an adult now and, at some point, if not now maybe soon, you will be sexually active.

That being said, not everyone has an open relationship with their parents. Some of you don't want to talk to your parents about your sex lives and some parents don't want to know. And some parents want to tell you more about sex (and their sex lives) than you'd ever want to hear. If sharing things like this with your family is hard or impossible, you can still talk to them about sex in terms of what it is like for your generation, so you can help them understand better what's real and true, and what's just a sensational story that the news media is touting. Keeping the communication lines open, even if you don't reveal everything, will show that you are being smart and honest, and hopefully it will lead them to better respect your privacy.

Part of what makes your parents hard to deal with is that they are afflicted with a sense of unrelenting anxiety for your safety. (If you find it annoying, imagine what it must feel like for them.) They felt it back when you were swinging on the monkey bars, and running by the pool, and they feel it today, say, if you're struggling in school. Sex is no different. Their fears will be about different things, depending on what their lives have been like and what they hear on the evening news. They'll worry about you contracting an STI, getting pregnant, and having your heart broken.

Some will even worry about what God or the neighbors think. Regardless of what exactly they worry about, they worry, and they don't stop worrying. That's their job — they just don't get paid for it.

Learning to educate your parents about your world and to communicate with them will help ease their worries. It's also vital if you want harmony (or just get through high school) while living in their house. Many parents welcome communication with their kids. If yours don't, remind them that it's been proven that teens who talk to their parents about sex are less likely to have unintended pregnancies. You can't learn everything from a book, not even this one.

HOW HAS SEX CHANGED?

You may think that sex is different today than it was in your parents' day, and this is what causes them to worry so much and misunderstand why you do the things you do. But has sex really changed?

Sex is sex. Beyond cyber sex, all of the sex we've been talking about in this book has been around since people have been having sex, which is a very long time. It may gross you out to know this, but your parents know what oral sex and vaginal sex and anal sex are. You don't need to educate them about those activities.

But some things have changed. For instance, the way we talk about sex has changed — society is a lot more open now than it used to be. Accep-

THEY'LL KILL ME

A lot of you might think your parents will kill you if you tell them that you are thinking about sex. Parents have a pretty solid investment in their kids, and they know that killing them would be as stupid as tricking out a race car, taking it to the track, then crashing it repeatedly into a wall. They are not only hoping you'll reach adulthood without burning down the house, but they're also looking forward to being taken care of by you and your lucrative career one day. Even if their faces turn all purplish and they start yelling, killing you is not an option.

WHAT IF I CAN'T TALK TO MY PARENTS?

OK, so your parents or guardians are not talking to you about sex. They won't talk to you about it even though you need to talk about it. Or they have talked to you, but only to tell you that you are too young to talk about it. Do you just rely on the info your friends or web pages give you? Since you likely have questions that are specific to you, it is a good idea to identify an adult you trust. This might be a teacher or another friend's older sibling or a parent.

tance of homosexuality has changed, and gay teens are more likely now to be open about their sexual orientation. Girls are no longer considered "ruined" if they lose their virginity before marriage. We also know more today about disease and how it is transmitted and how to protect ourselves. And we know more about how often sexual abuse occurs, which can better help us to prevent it. This is all positive stuff, and if your parents are in the dark about any of it, you can be the one to fill them in.

GAINING TRUST

Trust is one of the most difficult prizes to win at the carnival of the home. It sucks, but even when you exhibit the slightest bit of irresponsible behavior, it can result in your parents questioning how much they can trust you. If they don't trust you enough to leave you at home by yourself, they are certainly not going to trust you to have sex.

Here are some tips to gaining their trust:

- Do what you say you are going to do. If your parents can't rely on you to follow through with things you've said you will do or, worse, if they catch you in a lie — even once — earning their trust will be very hard.
- Be prepared to talk to them about sex. If you can't discuss it like a mature human being and can't say the words penis and vagina without busting into hysterical laughter (or tears), they are not going to think you are ready to have sex (and they are probably right).

- Educate yourself. Make sure you have all the facts about biology, birth control, and disease prevention before you talk to them. That will really impress them. Or, if you want to get that information from your parents, let them know you've done some research on your own and also want to hear their thoughts and opinions.

- Don't freak out. Even if your parents are being irrational, stay calm and try to continue the conversation as best as you can.

TALKING TO YOUR DOCTOR

Your doctor has the distinct privilege of getting to hear about and look at all sorts of interesting and sometimes gross things for a living. No matter how short a time they have been out of med school, your doctor is pretty well prepared for just about anything. Also, your doctor was once a teenager whose body went through changes and who thought about sex.

All of this is really just to say that you should feel comfortable telling your doctor what's going on with you. Part of the right of passage into doctorland is taking an oath to treat everyone equally. Doctors get paid to take care of you and you should help them do so by telling them the truth about important stuff like your sex habits, if you use drugs, and your favorite color. (That last one will lighten the mood in the office.)

If you want to talk to your doctor about stuff you don't want your parents to know, you should ask what his or her policies on confidentiality are beforehand. In many states, teens are protected by laws that allow them to tell their doctors things without their parents knowing. (This can get sticky when it comes to telling your doctor something that he or she considers to be a danger to you or other people. In that case they are required to do whatever they can to get you help and that would include telling your parents.)

If your parents come along, you could tell them that you would prefer to speak to your doctor confidentially during all or part of the visit. You can ask them ahead of time or just wait to ask them when you are there with your doctor.

If your parents or doctor will not respect your privacy, or if you don't like the vibe you get from your doctor, call your local Planned Parenthood or one of the other resources on pages 184-185 to inquire about other places to go.

TALKING TO THE OUTSIDE WORLD

Now that you know quite a bit about sex, we encourage you to take that knowledge and pass it on. It starts with your family and friends, but really there are tons of people out there who are either confused about sex or who think they know everything but have some pretty important things wrong.

A wonderful way to make a difference in the world of sexual information is to become what many universities and high schools call a peer adviser. This is when you take courses on helping other students with their questions. Each school's program (if the school has one) will be different, but the goal of helping to spread the knowledge is the same. There is also a cool website called Sexetc.org, which features content written by teens for teens.

If you are still wondering where you can personally get help with all of the issues bothering you, please check out the resources section that follows this chapter. It contains lots of great books, numbers, and websites that can help. •

Q & A

Q. I want to ask my boyfriend about his past sexual experiences, but every time I try to bring it up, he says we shouldn't talk about the past. I am scared he is hiding something. What should I do?

A. *This really all depends on what you want to know and why you want to know it.*

If you are really just interested in the basics — like if he's always had protected sex — you are smart to ask that information. Even though he may feel weird talking about it, explain to him that you want to be sure that the two of you make good choices when you have sex together. Assure him that you are not trying to judge him and that even if he has made mistakes it isn't going to make you angry. Prepare yourself for the answer, too. Be ready to hear whatever he has to say.

However, if you are asking him about his past relationships and sexual experiences in another way — because you want to know details of his personal life — it's really up to him whether he wants to share that. Try to remember that there is a reason he is not having sex with his ex anymore, and when he tells you that he doesn't want to talk about the past, it may be because it reminds him of something unpleasant. An important part of communicating is listening, and sometimes that means listening when someone says they don't want to talk about something.

It is also possible that his ex was the jealous type and she became upset after he spoke to her about other sexual experiences he'd had. Sometimes when people ask partners to tell them a little bit about their past loves or even flings, they get jealous and want to know more and more. Next thing you know, someone is stalking someone else's online profiles to look for past girlfriends. It can get very messy. If you are asking your boyfriend about his past sexual experience because you are jealous, you should back off. He is with you right now and you should enjoy the bond the two of you have and not dwell on his past.

Q. My boyfriend and I are ready to have sex, but we are not allowed to be alone in his room or mine with the door closed. We don't want to have sex in a car or something, but we don't know what to do. Help!

A. It's obvious that your parents are aware that you and your boyfriend want to have sex. They seem to think they can prevent that by keeping the doors open. So we know this sounds crazy, but perhaps you should talk to your parents and ask them about why it is they won't allow you private time with your boyfriend. See if you can ease some of their worries by telling them you are making conscious and safe decisions about having sex. (They'd also need to consider your boyfriend's parents because even if they consent to you having sex, they cannot make those choices for someone else's child.)

If talking to them doesn't work — or you know your parents well enough to know they'd never consent to you fooling around or having sex in the house — you may be tempted to have sex in cars or at other places like house parties. It's not ideal, but if you do that, always be safe and never have sex in public places or anywhere dangerous or secluded.

Q. My parents are stalking me. They have a record of every site I visit online, and they look at the texts on my phone and all my photos. What can I do to make them stop?

A. *Privacy is often a tough issue for teens and parents. Parents, especially these days, are paranoid about where their kids are going online, who they're talking to, and who they're texting. Again, it's all because they worry about you and the choices you're making. In this case, your parents seem particularly excessive with the monitoring, so maybe you need to sit them down, reassure them that you're being responsible, and ask them to cut you some slack and not read every email about who said what to whoever about whoever else. Remember that your parents are only taking part in this domestic espionage because they love you and they're concerned about you. Once you can prove that you're capable of making good decisions, probably they'll quit with the spying. If they don't, learn Morse code.*

Q. The last time I was at the doctor, she asked me if I was sexually active and I lied and said no. I am super careful about having safe sex. Do I really have to tell the doctor I am doing it?

A. *Being dishonest with your doctor won't do anyone any favors. Once you start having sex, your doctor needs to start performing exams differently and watching out for any abnormalities that may occur in even the most safe sex-having sex-havers. And if you ever do have an issue with your body that is related to sex, you want to have someone you can see about it.*

The question is: Why do you feel uncomfortable talking about sex with your doctor? If you think of sex as a thing to be ashamed of, you should confront those issues with a therapist or other trusted adult. If you simply don't trust your doctor, switch to a new one or visit a local Planned Parenthood (page 184) where you can be more open about your sex life.

Q. My mom walked in on me and my girlfriend having sex. My mom got really mad, and my girlfriend got so embarrassed that she refuses to ever come over to my house again. What can I do?

A. *You need to keep talking to both of them. Ask your mom why she is angry. If it is because she feels that you were doing something sneaky, work with her to re-establish a basis of trust. If she's freaked out that you are having sex, talk to her about it and try to address her concerns maturely.*

As for your girlfriend, try to be understanding. Imagine what it would feel like if one of her parents had walked in on the two of you. Keep reminding her that she didn't do anything wrong and that you care about her. Hopefully, one of these days, you three can find a way to laugh about it.

THERE ARE NO STUPID QUESTIONS — EXCEPT FOR THIS ONE

Q. My parents are really horrible at being parents, but my grandparents are really cool. Should I have a baby to kick-start my parents into the cool zone?

CHAPTER 12

SEX AND THE INTERNET

#StaySafe

This is a book about sex, and there's no way we can possibly talk about sex without talking about the thing that has had a huge impact on the way we pursue, understand, and even have sex. Since the earliest days of the internet, it was clear that the technology could be used to communicate with people you'd normally never have the opportunity to know. But even more remarkable was that you could also talk to people you would never have to meet in person or speak to again.

Partly as a result, the internet has contributed quite a bit to the contemporary idea of sex and sexuality. It's extremely easy to access porn (hooray!); it's also easier to distribute our own naked photos — or have naked photos distributed by others, even when we thought they were private (boo!); there are specialized message boards; we can all communicate instantly with almost whomever we want; and we can get information from experts or from idiots, depending on where we go. But the information is out there now and readily available, and that makes a big difference. Never again will we have to go through life pretending to know what a Cleveland Steamer is because we can find out in seconds at Urban Dictionary and elsewhere. (But then again, we might find our lives aren't really enriched by that knowledge.)

The point is, all of this technology has had a real impact, and that speed of change doesn't seem likely to slow down any time soon. Staying informed is a lot easier, but making sure you have the right information is a lot harder. So, lets talk about how to make all of this technology work best for you.

SOCIAL NETWORKS

Oh, good. You have the ability to tell everyone every single thought that ever pops into your head. And then, like magic, you get the instant gratification of comments, or of people "liking" what you do, or of people arguing with you over your taste in music. Hooray?

Well, however you feel about social media, it's out there, and you should feel free to post as little or as much as you'd like. However, you'll need to be savvy about the kinds of things you're posting. Here are some classic social network blunders you should steer clear of....

- **Oversharing:** While not the most terrible of all offenses, oversharing can often make people uncomfortable. It can also lead to people knowing things about you that you wish they didn't. So, before posting about your raging bladder infection, first consider all of the people who will read about it, now and in the future — and then decide if you really want to share.
- **Posting Provocative Pictures:** I know you're a hottie with a body and you want the world to know it. But you just shouldn't post pictures of you doing anything you don't want the world to see. You may think your privacy settings stop those photos from being seen by your grandma, but understand that anything you ever

put online might possibly make it to other websites that you don't have any control over.

- **Posting Illicit Behavior:** In case it needs to be said, don't do drugs. Don't drink if you're underage. That picture of Zack taking a bong rip at Becca's party is not going to do you any favors out in the world. And if you're of legal age, wasted pictures are rarely a good idea. One day you're in college, doing body shots and yelling, "Wooo!" and the next you've got a job as a middle school teacher and one of your students is sharing that photo with his friends. That story rarely ends well. So bear that in mind, because the past has a way of sticking around.

- **Righting a Perceived Wrong (Or Mourning a Break-up):** You're allowed to feel all the horrible things you're feeling when a relationship is over. However, that doesn't mean you should use the internet to talk smack about your ex. It's never pretty, even if he or she really did do something terrible.

CATFISHING

One of the most amazing things about life online is that you can be anyone you'd like. And, to a degree, nearly everyone has exaggerated something about himself or herself online.

Most of the time, it's completely harmless. Who really cares if you faked a British accent while playing an MMO? But creating a completely fictitious character in an effort to manipulate other people emotionally, physically, or financially is absolutely wrong and, in some cases, illegal. Just don't do it.

If you're talking to someone you suspect is a phony and it is important that you figure out if he's lying to you, you can use a reverse image searching tool to look up any photos he's using. You should also directly ask him. If it turns out you're wrong, you can just tell him he seemed too good to be true. If it turns out you're right, he'll usually disappear pretty quickly once he know you're onto him.

The most important thing to consider is that while most people out there aren't out to harm you, you should still always be smart. Don't give strangers your address or phone number. Don't use your real name in online forums. Create a secondary email account to use for people you don't know. This may all seem paranoid, but better safe than a headline.

CYBERBULLYING AND SEX

Anonymity often leads to bad behavior. People feel like it's okay to be complete turds to each other without ever having to consider that the person they're attacking is also a person. We're all expected to deal with this by developing thick skins and ignoring the amount of times we're insulted by people every day.

This behavior even extends itself to the people we know in real life. There have always been bullies and mean kids who would insult each other, spread rumors, and do a lot of needless name calling. Now that we're all online, that bullying has even more sticking power.

That kind of behavior has done incredible damage to many people across the world, and many of those episodes had to do with sex or sexuality. Kids who have trusted fake profiles to be real or bared their bodies online have been mercilessly shamed. People have secretly videotaped others and released the tapes, and sexuality has been outed and made fun of.

There is absolutely no reasonable way to place blame on the people who have been the victims. While at times they may have made unsafe choices online, what happened as a result is not their fault. The bullies who have backed these people into despair are completely responsible, and that kind of behavior must be stopped right away.

Every year, the laws around this type of crime are getting stricter, with more serious legal consequences. But even without the threat of fines or jail time, this is a trend that needs to stop. We have to learn that "Sticks and stones may break my bones but words will never hurt me." is absolutely incorrect. The words we use toward strangers, our friends, or the people we can't stand can be deadly and lead to irreversible consequences.

If you are being bullied IRL or online, you need to talk to someone before it becomes too much to handle. And, just as importantly, if you find that you are cyberbullying someone or multiple someones, you need help as well. There is something you aren't dealing with emotionally that is leading you to that kind of behavior, and it needs to be dealt with before you are responsible for causing someone else harm.

SAFETY

You're probably sick of hearing old people worry that you're going to get kidnapped if you talk to strangers online. Yes, every once in a while, bad things happen to people as a result of something directly related to technology. But, most of the time it doesn't. And that's why it's really easy to roll your eyes and disregard your grandfather's forwarded emails.

However, bad stuff does happen. Annoying stuff happens. And just plain weird stuff happens too. Some of that stuff is going to happen no matter what you do, but some of it can be avoided by taking precautions. Think of it like this: You can pay a health insurance company to help out in emergencies or help you when you're sick, but that doesn't mean you should be out there sticking nails in your eyes or gargling Ebola mouthwash.

So, what is considered dangerous online? Some of these things may seem really obvious, but if the ever-changing statistics are to be trusted, more than half of teens and young people are doing this stuff.

First, there are the sorts of websites you can visit that promote or encourage behavior that is destructive. Spending time at sites promoting anorexia, cutting, bulimia, self-harm, or other sites aimed at encouraging you to embrace harmful emotional and mental disorders is a terrible idea.

The same goes for participating in either posting videos or spending time watching videos/commenting on beat-down or other violent sites. Those people in those videos are real, and we have enough violence around us without further desensitizing ourselves with that kind of junk. You also could actually be putting yourself in legal trouble by taking part, even if all you did was watch the videos, because not reporting a crime is also a crime.

And, of course, most online activity has elements that could be dangerous. You're talking to strangers, posting personal information, getting caught up in a moment that could impact the rest of your life. We go into more details about that stuff, but honestly, your number one line of defense here is going to be your gut. Don't do any of the things we've already listed as dangerous behavior. But even if it didn't make the list, if your gut is telling you that something isn't right, even if you think you're overreacting, listen to yourself anyway.

As for actually meeting people in person, whether you're online dating or just chatting up strangers online for some anonymous sexy talk, understand that you don't know the people you are talking to. They could seem nice, and they might even be nice, but they also might have issues you don't know about. So, here are some simple things to keep in mind.

- **Don't give out your number:** Even if you're planning to meet the person, don't give it out until you're face-to-face with that person. Why? Well, first of all, because people can trace numbers. For a few bucks, they can do a public records search and find you. But also because what starts out as a few fun, romantic texts can soon turn into a neediness nightmare. You don't need anyone blowing up your phone at 2 am demanding where you are.
- **Don't give out passwords:** Seems like a really basic thing to remember. Of course you don't want anyone to know your passwords. But what if he wants to watch a movie you recommended and he doesn't have Netflix, so you think, "What harm could it do to just share my Netflix password?" Lots of harm, actually. Most people use the same kinds of passwords (even the same actual passwords, like "abc123," for instance), and it doesn't take an overly skilled hacker to try a combination of things to figure out how to get into any online account of yours he'd like to access.
- **Set up a dummy email account:** Your primary email account might not include your name, but if you've used that account to comment on things or buy things, or any number of other online

activities, it is really easy to figure out who you are, and as we already established, your anonymity is important.

- **Meeting for the first time:** Always do so in a public place. Always tell someone else where and when you're meeting him. Always have a back-up plan to get out. And never let him pick you up. This may seem overly cautious, but come on. It's just about being smart. The person you're talking to could seem excessively perfect for you, but he could show up and be nothing like you expected. He might not be a creepaziod spaz out to harm you, but he could just not be what you're looking for and be unable to take a hint.

SEXTING

All right. We may have already said this, but we really need to say it over and over. Do not take or let anyone take naked pictures of your before you're 18! Serious as a heart attack at a funeral, if you are under 18 and you're naked, be naked. Just don't photograph it, because there's no filter that will make getting busted for child pornography look any better.

Actually, a word to the wise: If you're 20 or younger, be sure you are very familiar with your state laws on all things related to sex, because they manage to really sneak some crazy crap in there.

Currently, all states consider any sexual or naked images of a person under the age of 18 to be "child pornography." So, if you're 17 and you snapped a booby selfie with your phone, you just created child pornography. And that's just the tip of the unsavory iceberg.

The laws around age of consent (how old you need to be to decide if you want to have sex) vary greatly from state to state. In some states, they even include language that takes into account that there may be a small age difference. What this means is that in some states, if you're 18 and you're having sex with someone who is 16, that might be legal. In other states, if you're 18 and having sex with a 17 year old, it's illegal. Those laws are broad and general and do not take individual maturity (or immaturity) into account.

In Massachusetts (and other states), the laws clearly lay out a variety of consequences for minors who participate in sexting. Like if you request a naked pic, you're on the hook for soliciting a minor. If you share naked pics that were sent to you, you're a distributor of kiddie porn.

The interesting (and troubling) thing about this whole mess is that the reason lawmakers are enforcing such strict policies around sexting is that they believe that by making these punishments severe, they will put an end to a behavior they think is dangerous. They're attempting to protect teens from the kind of trouble that can come out of snapping and sending naked pictures.

There are things that teens and children do need to be protected from. There are predators in life and online who are mentally ill and will do whatever it takes to convince underage people to engage in sexual behaviors with them. You have a right to be kept safe from those people, even when you are convinced that they're not doing anything wrong.

Unfortunately, what lawmakers are really doing with their crackdowns on "sexting" is adding danger to those activities by making them a crime. Know that you're taking a big risk by sexting if you're sending naked photos. Those photos can be shared, saved and exist somewhere forever, and even result in a felony conviction. So, put your top back on for a minute and go look up your state laws.

For the over-18 crowd, sending naked pictures can be a pretty cool way of letting someone know exactly what you think of him or her. But, before you get all sendy with the nudie pics, make sure to follow a few guidelines:

- **Ask if the receiver of the photos want them.** Some people aren't that into seeing your dong. Also, sending someone unwanted naked pictures of yourself can lead to that person sharing those pictures with others to tease you about it.
- **It's best to keep your face out of the pictures.** Faces are sexy on their own, and you can send some alluring shots of only your face, but once you hit send on a naked photo, it is out there forever.

- **Consider the person you're sending it to.** Would he or she share it with anyone? Would it upset you if he or she did? (Basically, don't send your pics to jerks.) There are websites entirely dedicated to people posting pictures without the other person's consent. Some of these sites are specifically for pictures and videos of exes, so even if you think the person you're swapping sexy pics with is in love with you, they might not always be.*
- **Consider what would happen if your photo was put online.** Would you lose your job? Would it dash your chances of being Miss America?

These sites are illegal, but they still exist. If you find yourself on one of these sites, even though you might feel ashamed, please step forward and contact the site administrators. You may need to get a lawyer involved. If you find your photo is on even one website, it might get posted in a lot of different places.

If you're asking for pics and the person you're asking says no, let it drop. It's very annoying to be constantly pestered to do something you're not comfortable with, and it can even be considered sexual harassment.

As for your own comfort, if you're trying to take sexy selfies to send to someone, don't get discouraged by photos that don't look amazing. It's not especially easy to get great angles, and your phone or computer's camera isn't exactly professional grade equipment, no matter what the commercials about it say.

ONLINE PORN

When it comes to online porn, everyone seems to have an opinion. Either porn is ruining our ability to have meaningful intimate relationships, or it's a healthy, safe sexual outlet. It's either a scourge on society, or it's completely harmless. Either way, the reality is that 90 percent of 8–16 year olds admit to having watched hard-core porn online. So, rather than act like your mom and go white as a sheet over it, let's talk about what it is that you're seeing.

You've probably heard this plenty of times, but we'll say it again. The people and scenes in professional adult films are not realistic expectations to set your sex-life by. Their bodies are often enhanced by plastic surgery, and there's a lot of behind-the-scenes preparation that you don't see. Real-life sexual encounters are oftentimes awkward and also require a level of safety you may not see online.

Also important to remember is that when you're actually having sex, you don't need to mimic what you saw online. The moaning, writhing, yelling out dirty talk — it can all actually ruin the mood by making things seem fake. Then there's the matter of how you treat the person you're having sex with. In porn scenes, people often degrade each other, spit, slap faces, cut each other off in traffic, and are generally pretty rude. Just because Anna Tripple Sexxxington Buttboobs (not a real porn name... yet) seemed to be into it, that doesn't mean your partner will want the same.

How you get your porn online is another matter. With so much access to free clips online, the porn industry has taken a blow. Some porn sites are set up so that you can get some things for free if you purchase full-length or high-def downloads. Be safe about giving out your financial information, read the fine print, and be wary of downloading file types you don't recognize.

With all of the talk about how porn isn't the same as reality, it can be easy to overlook something really important. Those little people living in your computer are real. They have families, they have friends, and they have feelings. They have hobbies and lives off-camera, and they don't deserve your ridicule. That's something to remember next time you find yourself itching to leave a terrible comment about them. Just because they are actors in the adult film industry, that does not make them any less valuable as people.

ONLINE (SEX) EDUCATION

The most difficult part of having so much access to information is that a lot of that information is total crap. You shouldn't base any reports on anything you find on Yahoo Answers, and you certainly shouldn't base your knowledge of sex on anything you find on Urban Dictionary.

One of the most frustrating things about being new to sex is the feeling that everyone else knows so much more about it than you do. Relax. Most people don't know very much but are too afraid to seem like they don't know.

Online information is often the blind leading the blind — except in this case, one of the blind people is claiming to have 20/20 eyesight. That's a great way to walk out into oncoming traffic. And since your secondary source of sex information is your group of friends, misinformation gets spread in two ways, and these ideas about sex that are incorrect become treated like realities. You'd probably tease your Aunt Edna for sending a warning email about a myth that could easily be disproved with a quick look on Snopes. And you should treat sex information the same way.

So, how do you know if the information you've found is accurate? Fortunately, there are some really great resources online, like Scarleteen.com, which will have answers to most, if not all, of your sex questions. And if you didn't find an answer, you could send in your question.

But other than just taking my word for it, how can you tell if the website you're looking at is any good? First, take a look at our special section in the back of the book where we list the best online resources out there (see pages 184-185). But should you stumble on a site with sex information, consider the following things:

Who is this information coming from?
- If it's a doctor, that doesn't always mean they're giving unbiased information. Take a moment to look up the doctor and see if he or she is actually a credible source.
- If it's not a doctor, that doesn't mean the information's wrong. There are websites like Sex, Etc. that are run by teenagers, but those teenagers are dedicated to giving accurate information through credible sources.

What is the information?

- Does it seem like it might be a lie or urban legend? Look it up and try to find a reliable source or two. Some weird stuff about sex turns out to be true, but most of the really weird stuff is just made-up nonsense.

- Is it written in a way that is meant to make you feel ashamed or somehow wrong for what you think or feel? Well, nobody needs that noise. Whenever you come across judgmental online information about your sexuality, move along. That's not even worth a troll's time.

WANNA BE AWESOME?

Let's say you've just come across some information online that you know is nonsense.

Maybe it's on some crowd-sourced site or it's the ranting of some lunatic. You can be a part of the solution. Comment, change Wikis, and show your sex smarts. By refuting someone's weird claim that douching with Gatorade prevents pregnancy, you could be providing a real service. Make sure to include links to fact-checked information. •

Q & A

Q. I'm a 16 year-old girl. My mom read my online chat between me and my girlfriend. I said things that I would never say in front of my mom, and now she will never look at me the same. Still, it wasn't right for her to invade my online privacy. How can I make sure she never does that again?

A. You can't. Sorry. This very same situation used to exist when parents would snoop on diaries or find notes in teens' pockets. If you're under 18, you have no privacy. That's just one of the many things that's totally unfair, but that's how it will always be. Except, in the case of the internet, your parent/guardian has even more reason to invade your privacy. That reason is a thing called "Parental Responsibility Law." Though each state has different versions of the law, it all boils down to the same idea: If you do something that causes trouble, your parents are responsible, too. (That doesn't mean you're off the hook, so don't go damaging public property just to get revenge on your mom.) Like it or not, it is your parent's job to know exactly what you are up to. And believe it or not, most parents hate having to snoop. It's about as much fun for your mom to know what you're into in the bedroom as it is for you to know what she's into.

Q. My boyfriend really likes watching porn, and it upsets me. I feel like he's cheating on me when he watches other women and masturbates. How can I make him understand and stop before it ruins our relationship?

A. First, let me say that it makes no difference what I define as cheating. Every relationship has its own rules and regulations. Sometimes you'll disagree, and sometimes those disagreements will be a big enough deal that you'll have to end the relationship. But let me try to help you see things a little bit differently.

Jealousy is a perfectly acceptable feeling. In your case, you are feeling jealous toward people who you and your boyfriend will most likely never meet or interact with at all. Again, normal. Too often people don't talk to each other about their jealousy because we've all heard a million times how terrible it is to feel jealous. Add that to the factor that you're feeling jealous over women who are a total abstract, and you probably feel like you need to label how you're feeling as anything else except jealousy.

Now that we've accepted that jealousy is normal and healthy, it's how you deal with that jealousy that could stand to be healthier. Yes, your boyfriend is watching naked women do sexual things. But what do you consider cheating, and does this really fall under that label? For many people, porn acts more like a visually stimulating masturbation aid. Consider this: Are you cheating when you use a vibrator?

I'd suggest that if you are interested in staying together with your boyfriend that you calmly have a discussion with him and talk out why it is that his porn-watching bothers you. I'd guess it stems from the normal stuff many other people feel. You don't want him to find anyone else more attractive than you. You don't want to compete with women whose job it is to look "perfect" naked. You feel like the things those women do in the sack are very different than what you and your boyfriend do. Whatever your reasons, if your boyfriend is worth a damn, he will be willing to listen to you and tell you the truth.

Q. My girlfriend wants to talk dirty over Skype, but I never know what to say. How do I make it sexy?

A. While it may seem like a terrifying task to come up with a bunch of ways to type sexy stuff that doesn't sound lame, think of it as an opportunity to mention your personal fantasies and to improve your one-handed typing skills.

Typically people think that they need to be in the moment by typing about what they are doing to the other person right then. It's actually way easier to start out by saying "This is what I wish we were doing right now." That way "I'm blanking your blank with my blank" doesn't seem so weird.

Start out with a fantasy or a scene you've watched or imagined, type a few sentences of that, and wait for her to reply. She might start steering things in a different direction, and together you two can create a shared version of your fantasy sex.

And remember to be polite. Just because you already finished doesn't mean the other person has.

Q. My boyfriend and I are both 19, and sometimes we talk dirty on the phone. He keeps sending me pictures of his penis. The problem is, I don't really like the pictures. They look gross to me. Does that mean I don't find him sexually attractive? And how can I tell him to stop without making him feel bad?

A. Traditionally speaking, I'd say you not wanting to see pictures of penises is fairly common. You can be totally attracted to a person and not want to look at pictures of his junk, even if it's a picture of his junk in a cool jacket and sunglasses.

Another fairly common thing is for people to get personal enjoyment from sending revealing pics of themselves to someone else. It can be exciting to think of someone else enjoying naked pictures of you. Unfortunately, it doesn't always work that way.

The best option, of course, is honesty. And that honesty doesn't have to (actually shouldn't) be that you are grossed out by his penis pics. Instead, say "I don't really like looking at naked photos. It's just not my jam."

Q. Is it okay to show friends pictures my girlfriend sent me?

A. No. It's not okay to show friends pictures anyone sent you without his or her permission. Even then, I advise against it. It may seem like you're just doing a little showing off, but when it comes to naked pictures, people get struck with the stupids and they can't keep their mouths shut. So, if you happen to be the recipient of a naked picture, let that be a pleasantly private thing between you and the sender.

RESOURCES

WEBSITES YOU SHOULD KNOW

Midwest Teen Sex Show
midwestteensexshow.com

That's our site! The series of three- to five-minute videos covers all sorts of sexual topics and will make you laugh.

Love, Sex, Etc.
milwaukeemagazine.com/lovesexetc

Nikol Hasler's weekly advice column. People of all ages send questions about sex and relationships, and sometimes even about losing their keys.

Planned Parenthood
plannedparenthood.org
800.230.7526

One of the United States' most valuable resources for health and sexuality concerns. This website offers a wealth of information. The clinics provide a variety of services, from testing and checkups to birth control, emergency contraception, and abortions.

Advocates for Youth
advocatesforyouth.org

This educational site gives you information about your rights as a teen and helps you make smart choices about sex.

Go Ask Alice!
goaskalice.columbia.edu

A Columbia University Q&A site that addresses all things related to sexual health.

Kinsey Confidential
kinseyconfidential.org

A sexuality information site for college-aged young adults designed by The Kinsey Institute for Research in Sex, Gender, and Reproduction™. Kinsey Confidential has articles, podcasts, and Q&As on sexual health.

San Francisco Sex Information
sfsi.org

A site run completely by volunteers who provide quick replies to all questions via email. This is the site that the MTSS sends teens to for questions about sexual health.

Scarleteen
scarleteen.com

This straightforward, nonjudgmental site about sex for teens was started by Heather Corrina. The MTSS refers to Scarleteen for good, solid sexual information.

Sex, Etc.
sexetc.org

A very cool resource that empowers youth to learn and teach. This site contains articles written by teens.

BOOKS YOU SHOULD READ

Our Bodies, Ourselves
by Boston Women's Health Book Collective

This book, which is about women's health issues, has been around since the

1990s and is constantly being updated. It is still a very useful book for anyone who knows someone with a vagina. Make sure to get the latest edition.

From The Inside Out: Radical Gender Transformation, FTM and Beyond
edited by Morty Diamond

This is a collection of stories from transgender females to males.

The New Male Sexuality, revised edition: The Truth About Men, Sex, and Pleasure
by Bernie Zilbergeld

Finally, a great book especially for boys about their sexual health.

Queer: The Ultimate LGBT Guide for Teens
by Marke Bieschke & Kathy Belge

Published by Zest, this awesome new quirky guide is a must-have for any LGBT teen and anyone who knows one.

LGBT RESOURCES

Gay & Lesbian National Hotline
www.glnh.org
888.843.4564

A hotline for gays and lesbians that offers one-on-one counseling over the phone as well as a list of local services in the US.

PFLAG (Parents, Families, and Friends of Lesbians and Gays)
pflag.org
202.467.8180

A useful site for gay youth and their friends and families, offering confiden-tial services related to health, educa-tion, and advocacy.

PLACES TO GO FOR HELP

America's Pregnancy Helpline
thehelpline.org
888.672.2296

A good number to call if you just need to talk about your pregnancy. It's a na-tional helpline, and the people on the phone will offer resources, information, and answer questions, but they will not attempt to make any decisions for you. They believe in offering information and support in a nonjudgmental way.

Centers for Disease Control STI Hotline
cdc.gov/STD
800.227.8922

A government-run, call-in program for information on STD clinic refer-rals, disease transmission, testing, and coping.

National Domestic Violence Hotline
ndvh.org
800.799.7233

A confidential number to call to get re-ferrals to services to help you deal with violence in your family or relationships.

Rape, Abuse, Incest National Network
rainn.org
800.656.4673

This is a place that does crisis interven-tion, ongoing support, and referrals to organizations that can help you if you were a victim of sexual assault, abuse, or incest.

INDEX

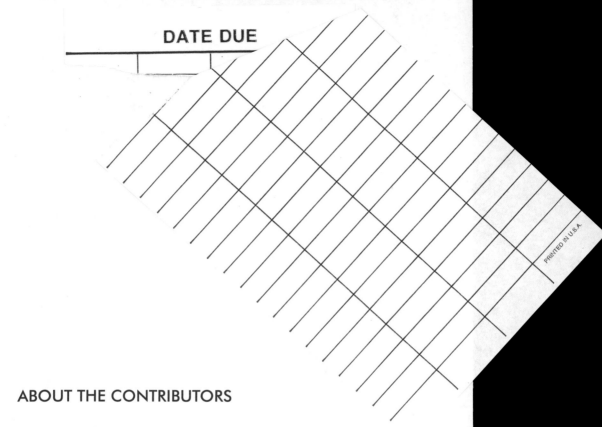
ABOUT THE CONTRIBUTORS

Nikol Hasler is a producer, writer, and project manager, as well as the ho
and writer of the successful web series *The Midwest Teen Sex Show*. She
currently lives in Los Angeles and works in public television. Her writing
has appeared in *Alternative Press*, *Glamour*, RHRealityCheck.org, and *The
Onion*'s A.V. Club, Chicago. She has given talks and facilitated workshops
about sex education at high schools and colleges, and via online forums.
She is an avid pickler and chef, and the mother of three sons.

Michael Capozzola is a San Francisco-based cartoonist, stand-up come-
dian, and creative consultant. His weekly cartoon, *Surveillance Caricatures*
appears in the *San Francisco Chronicle*. He's also illustrated for *National
Lampoon* and McSweeney's and has contributed premises to *Mad* magazine. He draws fast and has twice been called "unfailingly polite." Visit his
website at www.capozzola.com.